Meeting SEN
in the Curriculum:
MATHS

Other titles in the Meeting Special Needs in the Curriculum series:

Meeting Special Needs in English
Tim Hurst
1 84312 157 3

Meeting Special Needs in Modern Foreign Languages
Sally McKeown
1 84312 165 4

Meeting Special Needs in Citizenship
Alan Combes
1 84312 169 7

Meeting Special Needs in Religious Education
Dilwyn Hunt
1 84312 167 0

Meeting Special Needs in History
Richard Harris and Ian Luff
1 84312 163 8

Meeting Special Needs in Design and Technology
Louise Davies
1 84312 166 2

Meeting Special Needs in Art
Kim Earle and Gill Curry
1 84312 161 1

Meeting Special Needs in Music
Victoria Jacquiss and Diane Paterson
1 84312 168 9

Meeting Special Needs in ICT
Sally McKeown
1 84312 160 3

Meeting Special Needs in Science
Carol Holden
1 84312 159 X

Meeting Special Needs in Geography
Diane Swift
1 84312 162 X

Meeting Special Needs in PE and Sport
Crispin Andrews
1 84312 164 6

Meeting SEN
in the Curriculum:
MATHS

Brian Sharp

 David Fulton Publishers

David Fulton Publishers Ltd
The Chiswick Centre, 414 Chiswick High Road, London W4 5TF

www.fultonpublishers.co.uk

First published in Great Britain in 2004 by David Fulton Publishers.

Note: The right of Brian Sharp to be identified as the author of this work has been asserted by him in accordance with the Copyright, Designs and Patents Act 1988.

Copyright © Brian Sharp 2004

British Library Cataloguing in Publication Data
A catalogue record for this book is available from the British Library.

David Fulton Publishers is a division of Granada Learning, part of ITV plc.

ISBN 1 84312 158 1

Typeset by Servis Filmsetting Ltd, Manchester
Printed and bound in Great Britain by Ashford Colour Press

Contents

Foreword

For many years I was head of a mathematics department in a large comprehensive school. This book would have helped us a lot, not only because of all the information it provides about pupils with special educational needs in the context of mathematics, but also because of the sound practical advice it offers teachers seeking to provide *all* pupils with a good mathematical education. At the front of our departmental handbook we had this quote from George Polya's 1944 book, *How to Solve It*:

A teacher of mathematics has a great opportunity. If he fills his allotted time with drilling his students in routine operations he kills their interest, hampers their intellectual development, and misuses his opportunity. But if he challenges the curiosity of his students by setting them problems proportionate to their knowledge, and helps them to solve their problems with stimulating questions, he may give them a taste for, and some means of, independent thinking.

It was hard to live up to this challenge, but it was helpful to be continually reminded that we were aiming to develop the 'conjecturing atmosphere' which Brian describes so well (page 51).

In Chapter 4, Brian makes it clear that it is the right of all children, whatever their ability or disability, to experience the challenge of solving mathematical problems. He suggests that postponing problem solving until skills are secure is a big mistake. When children are struggling to solve problems for themselves, it is tempting for those working with them to make the strategic decisions for them and leave them merely to carry out the necessary calculations. When this happens, the calculations themselves present difficulties, whereas when pupils are involved in deciding for themselves the relevant problem-solving strategies, the calculations begin to make more sense (page 44).

This book offers sound advice to teachers about developing appropriate teaching and learning styles in the inclusive mathematics classroom – with practical strategies to help them develop good practice. So, if you are reading this book as the teacher with responsibility for SEN in your school, make sure the whole mathematics department reads at least Chapters 4 and 5. They will help staff to ensure that all pupils have a chance to become independent learners who are confident about the mathematics they have mastered.

Barbara Ball
September 2004

Acknowledgements

I am deeply grateful to the enduring love and tolerance of my wife, Sue, my sons, Jamie, Daniel and Connor and my parents, who have supported and encouraged me not only through writing this but throughout my career in education.

It has been, and remains, my privilege to work with many wonderful colleagues in schools – those who have influenced and developed my practice, and others who provided the sources of support necessary for us all to succeed. I give my thanks to all of them. They are: the friends and colleagues at Cedar School in Southampton, Ludlow CE School in Shropshire and Kingstone High School in Herefordshire. In particular, I would like to mention Brian Hart, Nigel Winter, Anne Henderson-Thynne, Margaret Jackson, Steve Byatt, Louise Sheppard, Sheila Poolton, Don Steward, Ashley Dowbiggin, Sallie Peacock, Trish Dugdale, Sara Longbottom and Ray Chatwin. I also wish to thank the teachers and teaching assistants at the schools in Herefordshire with whom I currently work.

Finally, but certainly not least, I wish to give my thanks to the many pupils who have both inspired and challenged me.

Contributors to the Series

The author

Brian Sharp works as the Key Stage 3 Mathematics consultant for Herefordshire. In this role he supports teachers in both mainstream and special schools throughout the county by sharing the planning, teaching and evaluation of lessons, and he leads courses in all aspects of mathematics at KS3. In the last year he has joined with a small group of consultants who have a particular interest in children with Special Educational Needs in a project led by the National Strategy team to develop materials nationally for teachers working in this area. Brian has a long experience of working both in special and mainstream schools as a teacher of mathematics. He has a range of management experience, including SENCO, mathematics and ICT co-ordinator. His MA is in Educational Management, for which he studied through the Open University.

A dedicated team of SEN specialists and subject specialists have contributed to the *Meeting Special Needs in the Curriculum* series.

Series editor

Alan Combes started teaching in South Yorkshire in 1967 and was Head of English at several secondary schools before taking on the role of Head of PSHE as part of being senior teacher at Pindar School, Scarborough. He took early retirement to focus on his writing career and has authored two citizenship text-books as well as writing several features for the TES. He has been used as an adviser on citizenship by the DfES and has emphasised citizenship's importance for special needs pupils as a speaker for NASEN.

SEN specialists

Sue Briggs is a freelance education consultant based in Hereford. She writes and speaks on inclusion, special educational needs and disability, and Autistic Spectrum Disorders and is a lay member of the SEN and Disability Tribunal. Until recently, she was SEN Inclusion Co-ordinator for Herefordshire Education Directorate. Originally trained as a secondary music teacher, Sue has extensive experience in mainstream and special schools. For six years she was teacher in charge of a language disorder unit.

Sue Cunningham is a Learning Support Co-ordinator at a large mainstream secondary school in the West Midlands where she manages a large team of Learning Support teachers and assistants. She has experience of working in both mainstream and special schools and has set up and managed a resource base for pupils with moderate learning difficulties in the mainstream as part of an initiative to promote a more inclusive education for pupils with SEN.

Sally McKeown is an Education Officer with Becta, the government funded agency responsible for managing the National Grid for Learning. She is responsible for the use of IT for learners with disabilities, learning difficulties or additional needs. She is a freelance journalist for the Times Educational Supplement and a regular contributor to disability magazines and to *Special Children* magazine. In 2001 her book *Unlocking Potential* was shortlisted for the NASEN Special Needs Book Award.

Subject specialists

English

Tim Hurst has been a special educational needs co-ordinator in five schools and is particularly interested in the role and use of language in teaching.

Science

Carol Holden works as a science teacher and assistant SENCO in a mainstream secondary school. She has developed courses for pupils with SEN within science and has gained a graduate diploma and MA in Educational Studies, focusing on SEN.

History

Richard Harris has been teaching since 1989. He has taught in three comprehensive schools, as history teacher, Head of Department and Head of Faculty. He has also worked as teacher consultant for secondary history in West Berkshire.

Ian Luff is Assistant Headteacher of Kesgrave High School, Suffolk and has been Head of History in three comprehensive schools.

Modern foreign languages

Sally McKeown is responsible for language-based work in the Inclusion team at Becta. She has a particular interest in learning difficulties and dyslexia. She writes regularly for the *TES*, *Guardian* and *Special Children* magazine.

Design and technology

Louise T. Davies is Principal Officer for Design and Technology at the Qualifications and Curriculum Authority and also a freelance consultant. She is an experienced presenter and author of award-winning resources and books for schools. She chairs the Special Needs Advisory Group for the Design and Technology Association.

Religious education

Dilwyn Hunt has worked as a specialist RE adviser, first in Birmingham and now in Dudley. He has a wide range of experience in the teaching of RE, including mainstream and special RE.

Music

Victoria Jaquiss is SEN specialist for music with children with emotional and behavioural difficulties in Leeds. She devised a system of musical notation primarily for use with steel pans, for which, in 2002, she was awarded the fellowship of the Royal Society of Arts.

Diane Paterson works as an inclusive music curriculum teacher in Leeds.

Geography

Diane Swift is a project leader for the Geographical Association. Her interest in special needs developed whilst she was a Staffordshire geography adviser and inspector.

PE and sport

Crispin Andrews is an education/sports writer with nine years' experience of teaching and sports coaching.

Art

Kim Earle is Able Pupils Consultant for St Helens and has been a Head of Art and Design. Kim is also a practising designer jeweller.

Gill Curry is Gifted and Talented Strand Co-ordinator for the Wirral. She has twenty years' experience as Head of Art and has also been an art advisory teacher. She is also a practising artist specialising in print.

ICT

Mike North works for ICTC, an independent consultancy specialising in the effective use of ICT in education. He develops educational materials and provides advice and support for the SEN sector.

Sally McKeown is an Education Officer with Becta, the government funded agency responsible for managing the National Grid for Learning and the FERL web site. She is responsible for the use of IT for learners with disabilities, learning difficulties or additional needs.

Contents of the CD

The CD contains activities and record sheets which can be amended/individualised and printed out for use by the purchasing institution.

Increasing the font size and spacing will improve accessibility for some students, as will changes in background colour. Alternatively, print onto pastel-coloured paper for greater ease of reading.

Introduction

All children have the right to a good education and the opportunity to fulfil their potential. All teachers should expect to teach children with special educational needs (SEN) and all schools should play their part in educating children from the local community, whatever their background or ability.

(*Removing Barriers to Achievement: The Government's Strategy for SEN 9*, February 2004)

A raft of legislation and statutory guidance over the past few years has sought to make our mainstream education system more inclusive and ensure that pupils with a diverse range of ability and need are well catered for. This means that all staff need to have an awareness of how children learn and develop in different ways and an understanding of how barriers to achievement can be removed – or at least minimised.

These barriers often result from inappropriate teaching styles, inaccessible teaching materials or ill-advised grouping of pupils, as much as from an individual child's physical, sensory or cognitive impairments: a fact which is becoming better understood. It is this developing understanding that is now shaping the legislative and advisory landscape of our education system, and making it necessary for all teachers to carefully re-consider their curriculum planning and classroom practice.

The major statutory requirements and non-statutory guidance are summarised in **Chapter 1**, setting the context for this resource and providing useful starting points for departmental INSET.

It is clear that provision for pupils with special educational needs is not the sole responsibility of the Special Educational Needs Co-ordinator (SENCO) and teaching assistants (TAs). If, in the past, subject teachers have 'taken a back seat' in the planning and delivery of a suitable curriculum for these children and expected the Learning Support department to bridge the gap between what was on offer in the classroom, lab or studio and what they actually needed – they can no longer do so. 'The Table of Roles and Responsibilities', Code of Practice (2002) states:

All teaching and non teaching staff should be involved in the development of the school's SEN policy and be fully aware of the school's procedure for identifying, assessing and making provision for pupils with SEN.

Chapter 2 looks at departmental policy for SEN provision and provides useful audit material for reviewing and developing current practice. The term 'special educational needs', or SEN, is now widely used and has become something of a catch-all descriptor – rendering it less than useful in many cases. Before the Warnock Report (1978) and subsequent introduction of the term 'special educational needs', any pupils who, for whatever reason (cognitive difficulties, emotional and behavioural difficulties, speech and language disorders), progressed more slowly than the 'norm', were designated 'remedials' and grouped together in the bottom sets, without the benefit, in many cases, of specialist subject teachers.

But the SEN tag was also applied to pupils in special schools who had more significant needs and had previously been identified as 'disabled' or even 'uneducable'. Add to these the deaf pupils, those with impaired vision, others with mobility problems, and even children from other countries, with a limited understanding of the English language – who may or may not have been highly intelligent – and you had a recipe for confusion, to say the least.

The day-to-day descriptors used in the staffroom are gradually being moderated and refined as greater knowledge and awareness of special needs is built up. (We still hear staff describing pupils as 'totally thick', a 'nutcase' or 'complete moron' – but, hopefully, only as a means of letting off steam!) However, there are terms in common use which, though more measured and well-meaning, can still be unhelpful and misleading. Teachers will describe a child as being 'dyslexic' when they mean poor at reading and writing; 'ADHD' has become a synonym for badly behaved; and a child who seems to be withdrawn or just eccentric is increasingly described as 'autistic'.

The whole process of applying labels is fraught with danger, but sharing a common vocabulary – and more importantly, a common understanding – can help colleagues to express their concerns about a pupil and address the issues as they appear in the classroom. Often, this is better achieved by identifying the particular areas of difficulty experienced by the pupil rather than puzzling over what syndrome this may be. The Code of Practice identifies four main areas of difficulty and these are detailed in **Chapter 3** – along with an 'at a glance' guide to a wide range of syndromes and conditions, and guidance on how they might present barriers to learning.

There is no doubt that the number of children with special needs being educated in mainstream schools is growing:

> because of the increased emphasis on the inclusion of children with SEN in mainstream schools the number of these children is increasing, as are the severity and variety of their SEN. Children with a far wider range of learning difficulties and variety of medical conditions, as well as sensory difficulties and physical disabilities, are now attending mainstream classes. The implication of this is that mainstream school teachers need to expand their knowledge and skills with regard to the needs of children with SEN. (Stakes and Hornby 2000:3)

The continuing move to greater inclusion means that all teachers can now expect to teach pupils with varied, and quite significant, special educational needs at some time. Even five years ago, it was rare to come across children with Asperger's/Down's/Tourette's Syndrome, Autistic Spectrum Disorder, or significant physical/sensory disabilities in community secondary schools. Now, they are entering mainstream education in growing numbers and all staff have to be aware of particular learning needs and able to employ strategies in the classroom (and lab, studio, gym) that directly address those needs.

Chapter 4 considers the components of an inclusive mathematics classroom and how the physical environment and resources, structure of the lesson and teaching approaches can make a real difference to pupils with special needs. This theme is extended in **Chapter 5** to look more closely at teaching and learning styles and consider ways in which to help all pupils maximise their potential.

The monitoring of pupils' achievements and progress is a key factor in identifying and meeting their learning needs. Those pupils who make slower progress than their peers are often working just as hard, or even harder, but their efforts can go unrewarded. **Chapter 6** addresses the importance of target setting and subsequent assessment and review in acknowledging pupils' achievements and in showing the department's effectiveness in value-added terms.

Liaising with the SENCO and support staff is an important part of every teacher's role. The SENCO's status in a secondary school often means that he/she is part of the leadership team and influential in shaping whole-school policy and practice. Specific duties might include:

- ensuring liaison with parents and other professionals

- advising and supporting teaching and support staff

- ensuring that appropriate Individual Education Plans (IEPs) are in place

- ensuring that relevant background information about individual children with special educational needs is collected, recorded and updated

- making plans for future support, and setting targets for improvement

- monitoring and reviewing action taken

SENCOs have invariably undergone training in different aspects of special needs provision and have much to offer colleagues in terms of in-house training and advice about appropriate materials to use with pupils. They should be a frequent and valuable point of reference for all staff, but are often overlooked in this capacity. Their presence at the occasional departmental meeting can be very effective in developing teachers' skills in relation to meeting SEN, making them aware of new initiatives and methodology and sharing information about individual children.

In most schools, however, the SENCO's skills and knowledge are channelled to the chalkface via a team of teaching or learning support assistants (TAs, LSAs). These assistants can be very able and well-qualified, but very underused in the classroom. **Chapter 7** looks at how teachers can manage in-class support in a way that makes the best use of a valuable resource.

Describing real-life situations with real pupils is a powerful way to demonstrate ideas and guidance. In **Chapter 8,** a number of case studies illustrate how different approaches can work.

The revised regulations for SEN provision make it clear that mainstream schools are expected to provide for pupils with a wide diversity of needs, and teaching is evaluated on the extent to which all pupils are engaged and enabled to achieve. This book has been produced in response to the implications of all of this for secondary subject teachers. It has been written by a mathematics specialist with support from colleagues who have expertise within the SEN field so that the information and guidance given is both subject specific and pedagogically sound. The book and accompanying CD provide a resource that can be used with colleagues to:

- shape departmental policy and practice for special needs provision

- enable staff to react with a measured response when inclusion issues arise

- ensure that every pupil achieves appropriately in mathematics

Meeting Special Educational Needs – Your Responsibility

Inclusion in education involves the process of increasing the participation of students in, and reducing their exclusion from, the cultures, curricula and communities of local schools.

(The Index for Inclusion 2000)

The Index for Inclusion was distributed to all maintained schools by the Department for Education and Skills and has been a valuable tool for many schools as they have worked to develop their inclusive practice. It supports schools in the review of their policies, practices and procedures, and the development of an inclusive approach and, where it has been used as part of the school improvement process – looking at inclusion in the widest sense – it has been a great success. For many people, however, the Index lacked any real teeth and recent legislation and non-statutory guidance is more authoritative.

The SEN and Disability Act 2001

The SEN and Disability Act 2001 (SENDA) amended the Disability Discrimination Act and created important new duties for schools. Under this Act, schools are obliged:

- to take reasonable steps to ensure that disabled pupils are not placed at a substantial disadvantage in relation to the education and other services they provide. This means that schools must anticipate where barriers to learning lie and take action to remove them as far as they are able;

- to plan strategically to increase the extent to which disabled pupils can participate in the curriculum, make the physical environment more accessible and ensure that written material is provided in accessible formats.

The reasonable steps taken might include:

- changing policies and practices
- changing course requirements
- changing the physical features of a building
- providing interpreters or other support workers
- delivering courses in alternative ways
- providing materials in other formats

Mathematics benefits from being a subject where its fundamental concepts can be presented in a range of ways: an arithmetic sequence can be understood from a series of numbers or a growing sequence of shapes; an understanding of bearings can be developed through physical movement or by examining points on a map. Thus, an understanding of mathematics is available to all.

See Appendix 2.1 for an INSET activity.

The Revised National Curriculum

The Revised National Curriculum (2002) emphasises the provision of effective learning opportunities for all learners, and establishes three principles for promoting inclusion:

- setting suitable learning challenges
- responding to pupils' diverse learning needs
- overcoming potential barriers to learning and assessment

The National Curriculum guidance suggests that staff may need to differentiate tasks and materials, and facilitate access to learning by:

- encouraging pupils to use all available senses and experiences
- planning for participation in all activities
- helping children to manage their behaviour, take part in learning and prepare for work
- helping pupils to manage their emotions
- giving teachers, where necessary, the discretion to teach pupils material from earlier key stages, providing consideration is given to age-appropriate learning context. (This means that a fourteen-year-old with significant learning difficulties may be taught relevant aspects of the Programmes of Study for mathematics at KS3, but at the same time be working on suitable material founded in the PoS for Key Stages 1 and 2. It is important to note that although some mathematical strands (e.g. algebra and probability) do not seem to appear until Key Stage 3, the foundations for understanding these are

being laid in Key Stage 2 – e.g. exploring number sequences, or finding fractions.)

The Qualifications and Curriculum Authority (QCA) has also introduced performance descriptions (P levels/P scales) to enable teachers to observe and record small steps of progress made by some pupils with SEN. These descriptions outline early learning and attainment for each subject in the National Curriculum, including citizenship, RE and PSHE. They chart progress up to NC level 1 through eight steps. The performance descriptions for P1 to P3 are common across all subjects, and outline the types and range of general performance that some pupils with learning difficulties might characteristically demonstrate. From level P4 onwards, many believe it is possible to describe performance in a way that indicates the emergence of subject-focused skills, knowledge and understanding. The DfES (0292/2002) text *Accessing the National Curriculum for Mathematics. Examples of what pupils with special educational needs should be able to do at each P Level* is discussed more fully in Chapters 4, 5 and 6.

The Code of Practice for Special Educational Needs

The Revised Code of Practice (implemented in 2002) describes a cyclical process of planning, target setting and review for pupils with special educational needs. It also makes clear the expectation that the vast majority of pupils with special needs will be educated in mainstream settings. Those identified as needing over and above what the school can provide from its own resources, however, are nominated for 'School Action Plus' and outside agencies will be involved in planned intervention. This may involve professionals from the Learning Support Service, a specialist teacher or therapist, or an educational psychologist, working with the school's SENCO to put together an Individual Education Plan (IEP) for the pupil. In a minority of cases (the numbers vary widely between LEAs) pupils may be assessed by a multi-disciplinary team on behalf of the local education authority whose representatives then decide whether or not to issue a statement

---

FUNDAMENTAL PRINCIPLES OF THE SPECIAL NEEDS CODE OF PRACTICE:

- A child with special educational needs should have their needs met.
- The special educational needs of children will normally be met in mainstream schools or settings.
- The views of the child should be sought and taken into account.
- Parents have a vital role to play in supporting their child's education.
- Children with special educational needs should be offered full access to a broad, balanced and relevant education, including an appropriate curriculum for the foundation stage and the National Curriculum.

of SEN. This is a legally binding document detailing the child's needs and setting out the resources which should be provided. It is reviewed every year.

Ofsted

Ofsted inspectors are required to make judgements about a school's inclusion policy, and how this is translated into practice in individual classrooms. According to Ofsted (2003) the following key factors help schools to become more inclusive:

- a climate of acceptance of all pupils;

- careful preparation of placements for pupils with SEN;

- availability of sufficient suitable teaching and personal support;

- widespread awareness among staff of the particular needs of pupils with SEN and an understanding of the practical ways of meeting these needs in the classroom;

- sensitive allocation to teaching groups and careful curriculum modification, timetables and social arrangements;

- availability of appropriate materials and teaching aids and adapted accommodation;

- an active approach to personal and social development, as well as to learning;

- well-defined and consistently applied approaches to managing difficult behaviour;

- assessment, recording and reporting procedures which can embrace and express adequately the progress of pupils with more complex SEN who make only small gains in learning and PSD;

- involving parents/carers as fully as possible in decision-making, keeping them well-informed about their child's progress and giving them as much practical support as possible;

- developing and taking advantage of training opportunities, including links with special schools and other schools.

Policy into practice

Effective teaching for pupils with special educational needs is, by and large, effective for all pupils, but as schools become more inclusive, teachers need to be able to respond to a wider range of needs. The Government's strategy for SEN (*Removing Barriers to Achievement* 2004) sets out ambitious proposals to 'help teachers expand their repertoire of inclusive skills and strategies and plan confidently to include children with increasingly complex needs'.

In many cases, pupils' individual needs will be met through greater differentiation of tasks and materials, i.e. school-based intervention as set out in the SEN Code of Practice. A smaller number of pupils may need access to specialist equipment and approaches or alternative or adapted activities, as part of a School Action Plus programme, augmented by advice and support from external specialists. The QCA, on its website (2003), encourages teachers: to take specific action to provide access to learning for pupils with special educational needs by:

(a) providing for pupils who need help with communication, language and literacy, through:

- using texts that pupils can read and understand
- using visual and written materials in different formats, including large print, symbol text and Braille
- using ICT, other technological aids and taped materials
- using alternative and augmentative communication, including signs and symbols
- using translators, communicators and amanuenses

(b) planning, where necessary, to develop pupils' understanding through the use of all available senses and experiences by:

- using materials and resources that pupils can access through sight, touch, sound, taste or smell
- using word descriptions and other stimuli to make up for a lack of first-hand experiences
- using ICT, visual and other materials to increase pupils' knowledge of the wider world
- encouraging pupils to take part in everyday activities such as play, drama, class visits and exploring the environment

(c) planning for pupils' full participation in learning and in physical and practical activities by:

- using specialist aids and equipment
- providing support from adults or peers when needed
- adapting tasks or environments
- providing alternative activities, where necessary

(d) helping pupils to manage their behaviour, to take part in learning effectively and safely, and, at Key Stage 4, to prepare for work by:

- setting realistic demands and stating them explicitly
- using positive behaviour management, including a clear structure of rewards and sanctions
- giving pupils every chance and encouragement to develop the skills they need to work well with a partner or a group

- teaching pupils to value and respect the contribution of others
- encouraging and teaching independent working skills
- teaching essential safety rules

(e) helping individuals to manage their emotions, particularly trauma or stress, and to take part in learning by:

- identifying aspects of learning in which the pupil will engage and planning short-term, easily achievable goals in selected activities
- providing positive feedback to reinforce and encourage learning and build self-esteem
- selecting tasks and materials sensitively to avoid unnecessary stress for the pupil
- creating a supportive learning environment in which the pupil feels safe and is able to engage with learning
- allowing time for the pupil to engage with learning and gradually increasing the range of activities and demands

Pupils with disabilities

The QCA goes on to provide guidance on pupils with disabilities, pointing out that not all pupils with disabilities will necessarily have special educational needs, and that many learn alongside their peers with little need for additional resources beyond the aids which they use as part of their daily life, such as a wheelchair, a hearing aid or equipment to aid vision. It states that teachers' planning must ensure, however, that these pupils are enabled to participate as fully and effectively as possible in the curriculum by:

- planning appropriate amounts of time to allow for the satisfactory completion of tasks. This might involve:
  - taking account of the very slow pace at which some pupils will be able to record work, either manually or with specialist equipment, and of the physical effort required;
  - being aware of the high levels of concentration necessary for some pupils when following or interpreting text or graphics, particularly when using vision aids or tactile methods, and of the tiredness which may result;
  - allocating sufficient time, opportunity and access to equipment for pupils to gain information through experimental work and detailed observation, including the use of microscopes;
  - being aware of the effort required by some pupils to follow oral work, whether through use of residual hearing, lip reading or a signer, and of the tiredness or loss of concentration which may occur.
- planning opportunities, where necessary, for the development of skills in practical aspects of the curriculum. This might involve:
  - providing adapted, modified or alternative mathematical activities or approaches to learning to enable pupils to make appropriate progress;

- providing alternative or adapted mathematical equipment for pupils who are unable to manipulate standard equipment or materials, or adapting the activities accordingly, e.g. by using dynamic geometry software to construct shapes instead of a compass, ruler and pencil.

- identifying aspects of Programmes of Study and attainment targets that may present specific difficulties for individuals. This might involve:
  - helping visually impaired pupils to learn about shape and space, through touch, movement or adapted visual resources;
  - providing alternative means of addressing mental tests for hearing impaired pupils.

Disapplication

Since mathematics is a fundamental way to describe our world, it follows that helping children to develop mathematical understanding is to empower them. There is, therefore, no case for disapplying children from the study of mathematics.

Summary

Pupils with a wide range of needs – physical/sensory, emotional, cognitive and social – are present in increasing numbers, in all mainstream settings. Government policies point the way, with inclusion at the forefront of national policy – but it is up to teachers to make the rhetoric a reality. Teachers are ultimately responsible for all the children they teach. In terms of participation, achievement, enjoyment – the buck stops here!

Departmental Policy

It is crucial that departmental policy describes a strategy for meeting pupils' special educational needs within the particular curricular area. The policy should set the scene for any visitor to the mathematics department – from supply staff to inspectors – and make a valuable contribution to the departmental handbook. The process of developing a department SEN policy offers the opportunity to clarify and evaluate current thinking and practice within the mathematics team and to establish a consistent approach.

The policy should:

- clarify the responsibilities of all staff and identify any with specialist training and/or knowledge;

- describe the curriculum on offer and how it can be differentiated;

- outline arrangements for assessment and reporting;

- guide staff on how to work effectively with support staff;

- identify staff training.

The starting point will be the school's SEN policy as required by the Education Act 1996, with each subject department 'fleshing out' the detail in a way which describes how things work in practice. The writing of a policy should be much more than a paper exercise completed to satisfy the senior management team and Ofsted inspectors: it is an opportunity for staff to come together as a team and create a framework for teaching mathematics in a way that makes it accessible to all pupils in the school.

Where to start when writing a policy

An audit can act as a starting point for reviewing current policy on SEN or to inform the writing of a new policy. It will involve gathering information and reviewing current practice with regard to pupils with SEN and is best completed by the whole of the department, preferably with some additional advice from the SENCO or another member of staff with responsibility for SEN within the school. An audit carried out by the whole department can provide a valuable opportunity for professional development if it is seen as an exercise in sharing good practice and encouraging joint planning. But before embarking on an audit, it is worth investing some time in a department meeting or training day, to raise awareness of special educational needs legislation and establish a shared philosophy. Appendix 2.1 contains overhead transparency (OHT) layouts and an activity to use with staff. (These are also on the accompanying CD, with additional exercises you may choose to use.)

The following headings may be useful in establishing a working policy:

General statement

- What does legislation and DfES guidance say?
- What does the school policy state?
- What do members of the department have to do to comply with it?

Definition of SEN

- What does SEN mean?
- What are the areas of need and the categories used in the Code of Practice?
- Are there any special implications within the subject area?

Provision for staff within the department

- Who has responsibility for SEN within the department?
- How and when is information shared?
- Where and what information is stored?

Provision for pupils with SEN

- How are pupils with SEN assessed and monitored in the department?
- How are contributions to IEPs and reviews made?
- What criteria are used for organising teaching groups?
- What alternative courses are offered to pupils with SEN?

- What special internal and external examination arrangements are made?

- What guidance is available for working with support staff?

Resources and learning materials

- Is there any specialist equipment used in the department?

- What physical, visual and aural mathematical resources exist in the department, and how are they matched to learning styles and needs?

- How are resources developed?

- Where are resources stored?

Staff qualifications and Continuing Professional Development needs

- What qualifications do the members of the department have?

- What training has taken place?

- How is training planned?

- Is a record kept of training completed and training needs?

Monitoring and reviewing the policy

- How will the policy be monitored?

- When will the policy be reviewed?

The content of an SEN departmental policy

This section gives detailed information on what an SEN policy might include. Each heading is expanded with some detailed information and raises the main issues with regard to teaching pupils with SEN. At the end of each section there is an example statement. The example statements can be personalised and brought together to make a policy. All the examples in this chapter are gathered as an example policy in Appendix 2.1.

General statement with reference to the school's SEN policy

All schools must have a SEN policy according to the Education Act 1996. This policy will set out basic information on the school's SEN provision: how the school identifies, assesses and provides for pupils with SEN, including information on staffing and working in partnership with other professionals and parents.

Any department policy needs to have reference to the school SEN policy.

Example

> All members of the department will ensure that the needs of all pupils with SEN are met, according to the aims of the school and its SEN policy.

Definition of SEN

It is useful to insert at least the four areas of SEN in the department policy, as used in the Code of Practice for Special Educational Needs.

TABLE 2.1 THE FOUR AREAS OF SEN

Cognition and Learning Needs	Behavioural, Emotional and Social Development Needs	Communication and Interaction Needs	Sensory and/or Physical Needs
Specific learning difficulties (SpLD)	Behavioural, emotional and social difficulties (BESD)	Speech, language and communication needs	Hearing impairment (HI)
Dyslexia	Attention Deficit Disorder (ADD)	Autistic Spectrum Disorder (ASD)	Visual impairment (VI)
Moderate learning difficulties (MLD)	Attention Deficit Hyperactivity Disorder (ADHD)	Asperger's Syndrome	Multi-sensory impairment (MSI)
Severe learning difficulties (SLD)			Physical difficulties (PD)
Profound and multiple learning difficulties (PMLD)			Other

Provision for staff within the department

In many schools, each department nominates a member of staff to have special responsibility for SEN provision (with or without remuneration). This can be very effective where there is a system of regular liaison between department SEN representatives and the SENCO in the form of meetings or paper communications or a mixture of both.

The responsibilities of this post may include liaison between the department and the SENCO, attending any liaison meetings and providing feedback via meetings and minutes, attending training, maintaining the departmental SEN information and records and representing the needs of pupils with SEN at departmental level. This post can be seen as a valuable development opportunity for staff. The name of this person should be included in the policy.

How members of the department raise concerns about pupils with SEN can be included in this section. Concerns may be raised at specified departmental meetings before referral to the SENCO. An identified member of the department could make referrals to the SENCO and keep a record of this information.

Reference to working with support staff will include a commitment to planning and communication between staff. There may be information on inviting support staff to meetings, resources and lesson plans.

A reference to the centrally held lists of pupils with SEN and other relevant information will also be included in this section. A note about confidentiality of information should be included.

Example

> The member of staff with responsibility for overseeing the provision of SEN within the department will attend liaison meetings and feed back to other members of the department. They will maintain the department's SEN information file, attend appropriate training and disseminate this to all departmental staff. All information will be treated with confidentiality.

Provision for pupils with SEN

It is the responsibility of all staff to know which pupils have SEN and to identify any pupils having difficulties. Pupils with SEN may be identified by staff within the department in a variety of ways; these may be listed and could include:

- observation in lessons
- assessment of class work
- homework tasks
- end of module tests
- progress checks

- annual examinations

- reports

Setting out how pupils with SEN are grouped within the mathematics department may include specifying the criteria used and/or the philosophy behind the method of grouping.

Example

> The pupils are grouped according to ability as informed by Key Stage 2 results, reading scores and any other relevant performance, social or medical information.
>
> Monitoring arrangements and details of how pupils can move between groups should also be set out. Information collected may include:
>
> - National Curriculum levels
>
> - departmental assessments
>
> - reading scores
>
> - advice from pastoral staff
>
> - discussion with staff in the SEN department
>
> - information provided on IEPs

Special examination arrangements need to be considered not only at Key Stages 3 and 4 but also for internal examinations. How and when these will be discussed should be clarified. Reference to SENCO and examination arrangements from the examination board should be taken into account. Ensuring that staff in the department understand the current legislation and guidance from central government is important, so a reference to the SEN Code of Practice and the levels of SEN intervention is helpful within the policy. Here is a good place also to put a statement about the school behaviour policy and rewards and sanctions, and how the department will make any necessary adjustments to meet the needs of pupils with SEN.

Example

> It is understood that pupils with SEN may receive additional support if they have a statement of SEN, are at School Action or School Action Plus. The staff in the mathematics department will aim to support the pupils to achieve their targets as specified on their IEPs and will provide feedback for IEP or statement reviews. Pupils with SEN will be included in the departmental monitoring system used for all pupils. Additional support will be requested as appropriate.

Resources and learning materials

The department policy needs to specify what differentiated materials are available, where they are kept and how to find new resources. This section could include a statement about working with support staff to develop resources or access specialist resources as needed, and the use of ICT. Teaching strategies may also be identified if appropriate. Advice on more specialist equipment can be sought as necessary, possibly through LEA support services: contact details may be available from the SENCO, or the department may have direct links. Any specially bought subject text or alternative/appropriate courses can be specified as well as any external assessment and examination courses.

Example

The department will provide suitably differentiated materials and, where appropriate, specialist resources for pupils with SEN. Additional texts are available for those pupils working below National Curriculum level 3. At Key Stage 4 an alternative course to GCSE is offered at Entry level but, where possible, pupils with SEN will be encouraged to reach their full potential and follow a GCSE course. Support staff will be provided with curriculum information in advance of lessons and will also be involved in lesson planning. A list of resources is available in the department handbook and on the noticeboard.

Staff qualifications and Continuing Professional Development needs

It is important to recognise and record the qualifications and special skills gained by staff within the department. Training can include not only external courses but also in-house INSET and opportunities such as observing other staff, working to produce materials with other staff, and visiting other establishments. Staff may have hidden skills that might enhance the work of the department and the school, e.g. some staff might be proficient in the use of sign language.

Example

A record of training undertaken, specialist skills and training required will be kept in the department handbook. Requests for training will be considered in line with the department and school improvement plan.

Monitoring and reviewing the policy

To be effective any policy needs regular monitoring and review. These can be planned as part of the yearly cycle. The responsibility for the monitoring can rest with the Head of Department but will have more effect if supported by someone from outside acting as a critical friend. This could be the SENCO or a member of the senior management team in school.

Example

> The department SEN policy will be monitored by the Head of Department on a planned annual basis, with advice being sought from the SENCO as part of a three-yearly review process.

Summary

Creating a departmental SEN policy should be a developmental activity to improve the teaching and learning for all pupils but especially those with special or additional needs. The policy should be a working document that will evolve and change; it is there to challenge current practice and to encourage improvement for both pupils and staff. If departmental staff work together to create the policy, they will have ownership of it; it will have true meaning and be effective in clarifying practice.

Different Types of SEN

This chapter is a starting point for information on the special educational needs most frequently occurring in the mainstream secondary school. It describes the main characteristics of each learning difficulty with practical ideas for use in subject areas, and contacts for further information. Some of the tips are based on good secondary practice while others encourage teachers to try new or less familiar approaches.

The special educational needs outlined in this chapter are grouped under the headings used in the SEN Code of Practice (DfES 2001):

- cognition and learning

- behavioural, emotional and social development

- communication and interaction

- sensory and/or physical needs

(See Table 2.1 in chapter 2.)

The labels used in this chapter are useful when describing pupils' difficulties, but it is important to remember not to use the label in order to define the pupil. Put the pupil before the difficulty, saying 'the pupil with special educational needs' rather than 'the SEN pupil', 'pupils with MLD' rather than 'MLDs'.

Remember to take care in using labels when talking with parents, pupils or other professionals. Unless a pupil has a firm diagnosis, and parents and pupil understand the implications of that diagnosis, it is more appropriate to describe the features of the special educational need rather than use the label. For example, a teacher might describe a pupil's spelling difficulties but not use the term 'dyslexic'.

The number and profile of pupils with special educational needs will vary from school to school, so it is important to consider the pupil with SEN as an individual within your school and subject environment. The strategies contained in this chapter will help teachers adapt that environment to meet the needs of individual pupils within the subject context. For example, rather than saying 'He can't read the worksheet', recognise that the worksheet is too difficult for the pupil, and adapt the work accordingly.

There is a continuum of need within each of the special educational needs listed here. Some pupils will be affected more than others, and show fewer or more of the characteristics described.

The availability and levels of support from professionals within a school (e.g. SENCOs, support teachers, Teaching Assistants (TAs)) and external professionals (e.g. educational psychologists, Learning Support Service staff and medical staff) will depend on the severity of pupils' SEN. This continuum of need will also impact on the subject teacher's planning and allocation of support staff.

Pupils with other, less common special educational needs may be included in some secondary schools, and additional information on these conditions may be found in a variety of sources. These include the school SENCO, LEA support services, educational psychologists and the Internet.

Asperger's Syndrome

Asperger's Syndrome is a disorder at the able end of the autistic spectrum. People with Asperger's Syndrome have average to high intelligence but share the same Triad of Impairments. They often want to make friends but do not understand the complex rules of social interaction. They have impaired fine and gross motor skills, with writing being a particular problem. Boys are more likely to be affected – with the ratio being 10:1 boys to girls. Because they appear 'odd' and naïve, these pupils are particularly vulnerable to bullying.

Main characteristics:

- **Social interaction**
  Pupils with Asperger's Syndrome want friends but have not developed the strategies necessary for making and sustaining friendships. They find it very difficult to learn social norms and to pick up on social cues. Highly social situations, such as lessons, can cause great anxiety.

- **Social communication**
  Pupils have appropriate spoken language but tend to sound formal and pedantic, using little expression and with an unusual tone of voice. They have difficulty using and understanding non-verbal language such as facial expression, gesture, body language and eye contact. They have a literal understanding of language and do not grasp implied meanings.

- **Social imagination**
  Pupils with Asperger's Syndrome need structured environments, and to have routines they understand and can anticipate. They excel at learning facts and figures, but have difficulty understanding abstract concepts and in generalising information and skills. They often have all-consuming special interests.

How can the subject teacher help?

- Liaise closely with parents, especially over homework.
- Create as calm a classroom environment as possible.
- Allow to sit in the same place for each lesson.
- Set up a work buddy system for your lessons.
- Provide additional visual cues in class.
- Give time to process questions and respond.
- Make sure pupils understand what to do.
- Allow alternatives to writing for recording.
- Use visual timetables and task activity lists.
- Prepare for changes to routines well in advance.
- Give written homework instructions and stick into an exercise book.
- Have your own class rules and apply them consistently.

The National Autistic Society, 393 City Road, London ECIV 1NG
Tel: 0845 070 4004 Helpline (10am–4pm, Mon–Fri)
Tel: 020 7833 2299 Fax: 020 7833 9666
Email: nas@nas.org.uk Website: http://www.nas.org.uk

Attention Deficit Disorder (with or without hyperactivity) (ADD/ADHD)

Attention Deficit Hyperactivity Disorder is a term used to describe children who exhibit over-active behaviour and impulsivity and who have difficulty in paying attention. It is caused by a form of brain dysfunction of a genetic nature. ADHD can sometimes be controlled effectively by medication. Children of all levels of ability can have ADHD.

Main characteristics:

- difficulty in following instructions and completing tasks
- easily distracted by noise, movement of others, objects attracting attention
- often doesn't listen when spoken to
- fidgets and becomes restless, can't sit still
- interferes with other pupils' work
- can't stop talking, interrupts others, calls out
- runs about when inappropriate
- has difficulty in waiting or taking turns
- acts impulsively without thinking about the consequences

How can the subject teacher help?

- Make eye contact and use the pupil's name when speaking to him.
- Keep instructions simple – the one sentence rule.
- Provide clear routines and rules, and rehearse them regularly.
- Sit the pupil away from obvious distractions, e.g. windows, the computer.
- In busy situations direct the pupil by name to visual or practical objects.
- Encourage the pupil to repeat back instructions before starting work.
- Tell the pupil when to begin a task.
- Give two choices – avoid the option of the pupil saying 'No' by asking, 'Do you want to write in blue or black pen?'
- Give advanced warning when something is about to happen. Change or finish with a time, e.g. 'In two minutes I need you (pupil name) to . . . '
- Give specific praise – catch them being good, give attention for positive behaviour.
- Give the pupil responsibilities so that others can see them in a positive light and the pupil develops a positive self-image.

ADD Information Services, PO Box 340, Edgware, Middlesex HA8 9HL
Tel: 020 8906 9068
ADDNET UK Website: www.btinternet.com/~black.ice/addnet/

Autistic Spectrum Disorders (ASD)

The term 'Autistic Spectrum Disorders' is used for a range of disorders affecting the development of social interaction, social communication, and social imagination and flexibility of thought. This is known as the 'Triad of Impairments'. Pupils with ASD cover the full range of ability, and the severity of the impairment varies widely. Some pupils also have learning disabilities or other difficulties. Four times as many boys as girls are diagnosed with an ASD.

Main characteristics:

- **Social interaction**
  Pupils with an ASD find it difficult to understand social behaviour and this affects their ability to interact with children and adults. They do not always understand social contexts. They may experience high levels of stress and anxiety in settings that do not meet their needs or when routines are changed. This can lead to inappropriate behaviour.

- **Social communication**
  Understanding and use of non-verbal and verbal communication are impaired. Pupils with an ASD have difficulty understanding the communication of others and in developing effective communication themselves. They have a literal understanding of language. Many are delayed in learning to speak, and some never develop speech at all.

- **Social imagination and flexibility of thought**
  Pupils with an ASD have difficulty in thinking and behaving flexibly which may result in restricted, obsessional, or repetitive activities. They are often more interested in objects than people, and have intense interests in one particular area, such as trains or vacuum cleaners. Pupils work best when they have a routine. Unexpected changes in those routines will cause distress. Some pupils with Autistic Spectrum Disorders have a different perception of sounds, sights, smell, touch, and taste, and this can affect their response to these sensations.

How can subject teachers help?

- Liaise with parents as they will have many useful strategies.
- Provide visual supports in class: objects, pictures, etc.
- Give a symbolic or written timetable for each day.
- Give advance warning of any changes to usual routines.
- Provide either an individual desk or with a work buddy.
- Avoid using too much eye contact as it can cause distress.
- Give individual instructions using the pupil's name, e.g. 'Paul, bring me your book.'
- Allow access to computers.
- Develop social interactions using a buddy system or Circle of Friends.
- Avoid using metaphor, idiom or sarcasm – use simple language.
- Use special interests to motivate.
- Allow difficult situations to be rehearsed by means of Social Stories.

BEHAVIOURAL, EMOTIONAL AND SOCIAL DEVELOPMENT NEEDS

This term includes behavioural, emotional and social difficulties and Attention Deficit Disorder with or without hyperactivity. These difficulties can be seen across the whole ability range and have a continuum of severity. Pupils with special educational needs in this category are those who have persistent difficulties despite an effective school behaviour policy and a personal and social curriculum.

Behavioural, emotional and social difficulties (BESD)

Main characteristics:

- inattentive, poor concentration and lack of interest in school/school work
- easily frustrated, anxious about changes
- unable to work in groups
- unable to work independently, constantly seeking help
- confrontational – verbally aggressive towards pupils and/or adults
- physically aggressive towards pupils and/or adults
- destroys property – their own/others
- appears withdrawn, distressed, unhappy, sulky, may self-harm
- lacks confidence, acts extremely frightened, lacks self-esteem
- finds it difficult to communicate
- finds it difficult to accept praise

How can the subject teacher help?

- Check the ability level of the pupil and adapt the level of work to this.
- Consider the pupil's strengths and use them.
- Tell the pupil what you expect in advance, as regards work and behaviour.
- Talk to the pupil to find out a bit about them.
- Set a subject target with a reward system.
- Focus your comments on the behaviour not on the pupil and offer an alternative way of behaving when correcting the pupil.
- Use positive language and verbal praise whenever possible.
- Tell the pupil what you want them to do: 'I need you to . . . , I want you to . . .' rather than ask. This avoids confrontation and allows the possibility that there is room for negotiation.
- Give the pupil a choice between two options.
- Stick to what you say.
- Involve the pupil in responsibilities to increase self-esteem and confidence.
- Plan a 'time out' system. Ask a colleague for help with this.

SEBDA is the new name for the Association of Workers for Children with Emotional and Behavioural Difficulties.
Website: www.awcebd.co.uk

Cerebral palsy (CP)

Cerebral palsy is a persistent disorder of movement and posture. It is caused by damage or lack of development to part of the brain before or during birth or in early childhood. Problems vary from slight clumsiness to more severe lack of control of movements. Pupils with CP may also have learning difficulties. They may use a wheelchair or other mobility aid.

Main characteristics:

There are three main forms of cerebral palsy:

- *spasticity* – disordered control of movement associated with stiffened muscles

- *athetosis* – frequent involuntary movements

- *ataxia* – an unsteady gait with balance difficulties and poor spatial awareness

   Pupils may also have communication difficulties.

How can the subject teacher help?

- Talk to parents, the physiotherapist – and the pupil.

- Consider the classroom layout.

- Have high academic expectations.

- Use visual supports: objects, pictures, symbols.

- Arrange a work/subject buddy.

- Speak directly to the pupil rather than through a TA.

- Ensure access to appropriate IT equipment for the subject – and that it is used.

Scope, PO Box 833, Milton Keynes MK12 5NY
Tel: 0808 800 3333 (Freephone helpline) Fax: 01908 321051
Email: cphelpline@scope.org.uk   Website: http://www.scope.org.uk

Down's Syndrome (DS)

Down's Syndrome is the most common identifiable cause of learning disability. This is a genetic condition caused by the presence of an extra chromosome 21. People with DS have varying degrees of learning difficulties ranging from mild to severe. They have a specific learning profile with characteristic strengths and weaknesses. All have certain physical characteristics but will also inherit family traits, in physical features and personality. They may have additional sight, hearing, respiratory and heart problems.

Main characteristics:

- delayed motor skills
- take longer to learn and consolidate new skills
- limited concentration
- difficulties with generalisation, thinking and reasoning
- sequencing difficulties
- stronger visual than aural skills
- better social than academic skills

How can the subject teacher help?

- Ensure that the pupil can see and hear you and other pupils.
- Speak directly to the pupil and reinforce with facial expression, pictures and objects.
- Use simple, familiar language in short sentences.
- Check instructions have been understood.
- Give time for the pupil to process information and formulate a response.
- Break lessons up into a series of shorter, varied and achievable tasks.
- Accept other ways of recording: drawings, tape/video recordings, symbols, etc.
- Set differentiated tasks linked to the work of the rest of the class.
- Provide age-appropriate resources and activities.
- Allow working in top sets to give good behaviour models.
- Provide a work buddy.
- Expect unsupported work for part of each lesson.

The Down's Association, 155 Mitcham Road, London SW17 9PG
Tel: 0845 230 0372
Email: info@downs-syndrome.org.uk
Website: http://www.downs-syndrome.org.uk

Fragile X Syndrome

Fragile X Syndrome is caused by a malformation of the X chromosome and is the most common form of inherited learning disability. This intellectual disability varies widely, with up to a third having learning problems ranging from moderate to severe. More boys than girls are affected but both may be carriers.

Main characteristics:

- delayed and disordered speech and language development
- difficulties with the social use of language
- articulation and/or fluency difficulties
- verbal skills better developed than reasoning skills
- repetitive or obsessive behaviour, such as hand-flapping, chewing, etc.
- clumsiness and fine motor co-ordination problems
- attention deficit and hyperactivity
- easily anxious or overwhelmed in busy environments

How can the subject teacher help?

- Liaise with parents.
- Make sure the pupil knows what is to happen in each lesson – provide visual timetables, work schedules or written lists.
- Ensure the pupil sits at the front of the class, in the same seat for all lessons.
- Arrange a work/subject buddy.
- Where possible keep to routines and give prior warning of all changes.
- Make instructions clear and simple.
- Use visual supports: objects, pictures, symbols.
- Allow the pupil to use a computer to record and access information.
- Give lots of praise and positive feedback.

Fragile X Society, Rood End House, 6 Stortford Road, Dunmow, Essex CM6 1DA
Tel: 01424 813147 (Helpline) Tel: 01371 875100 (Office)
Email: info@fragilex.org.uk Website: http://www.fragilex.org.uk

Moderate Learning Difficulties (MLD)

The term 'moderate learning difficulties' is used to describe pupils who find it extremely difficult to achieve expected levels of attainment across the curriculum, even with a differentiated and flexible approach. These pupils do not find learning easy and can suffer from low self-esteem and sometimes exhibit unacceptable behaviour as a way of avoiding failure.

Main characteristics:

- difficulties with reading, writing and comprehension
- unable to understand and retain basic mathematical skills and concepts
- immature social and emotional skills
- limited vocabulary and communication skills
- short attention span
- under-developed co-ordination skills
- lack of logical reasoning
- inability to transfer and apply skills to different situations
- difficulty remembering what has been taught
- difficulty with organising themselves, following a timetable, remembering books and equipment

How can the subject teacher help?

- Check the pupil's strengths, weaknesses and attainment levels.
- Establish a routine within the lesson.
- Keep tasks short and varied.
- Keep listening tasks short or broken up with activities.
- Provide word lists, writing frames, shorten text.
- Try alternative methods of recording information, e.g. drawings, charts, labelling, diagrams, use of ICT.
- Check previously gained knowledge and build on this.
- Repeat information in different ways.
- Show the child what to do or what the expected outcome is; demonstrate or show examples of completed work.
- Use practical, concrete, visual examples to illustrate explanations.
- Question the pupil to check they have grasped a concept or can follow instructions.
- Make sure the pupil always has something to do.
- Use lots of praise, instant rewards – catch them trying hard.

The MLD Alliance, c/o The Elfrida Society, 34 Islington Park Street, London N1 1PX
Website: www.mldalliance.com/executive.htm

Physical Disability (PD)

There is a wide range of physical disabilities (PD), and pupils with PD cover all academic abilities. Some pupils are able to access the curriculum and learn effectively without additional educational provision. They have a disability but do not have a special educational need. For other pupils, the impact on their education may be severe, and the school will need to make adjustments to enable them to access the curriculum.

Some pupils with a physical disability have associated medical conditions which may impact on their mobility. These include cerebral palsy, heart disease, spina bifida and hydrocephalus, and muscular dystrophy. Pupils with physical disabilities may also have sensory impairments, neurological problems or learning difficulties. They may use a wheelchair and/or additional mobility aids. Some pupils will be mobile but may have significant fine motor difficulties that require support. Others may need augmentative or alternative communication aids.

Pupils with a physical disability may need to miss lessons to attend physiotherapy or medical appointments. They are also likely to become very tired as they expend greater effort to complete everyday tasks. Schools will need to be flexible and sensitive to individual pupil needs.

How can the subject teacher help?

- Get to know pupils and parents and they will help you make the right adjustments.

- Maintain high expectations.

- Consider the classroom layout.

- Allow the pupil to leave lessons a few minutes early to avoid busy corridors and give time to get to the next lesson.

- Set homework earlier in the lesson so instructions are not missed.

- Speak directly to the pupil rather than through a TA.

- Let pupils make their own decisions.

- Ensure access to appropriate IT equipment for the lesson – and that it is used!

- Give alternative ways of recording work.

- Plan to cover work missed through medical or physiotherapy appointments.

- Be sensitive to fatigue, especially at the end of the school day.

Semantic Pragmatic Disorder (SPD)

Semantic Pragmatic Disorder is a communication disorder which falls within the autistic spectrum. 'Semantic' refers to the meanings of words and phrases and 'pragmatic' refers to the use of language in a social context. Pupils with this disorder have difficulties understanding the meaning of what people say and in using language to communicate effectively. Pupils with SPD find it difficult to extract the central meaning – saliency – of situations.

Main characteristics:

- delayed language development

- fluent speech but may sound stilted or over-formal

- may repeat phrases out of context from videos or adult conversations

- difficulty understanding abstract concepts

- limited or inappropriate use of eye contact, facial expression or gesture

- motor skills problems

How can the subject teacher help?

- Sit the pupil at the front of the room to avoid distractions.

- Use visual supports: objects, pictures, symbols.

- Pair with a work/subject buddy.

- Create a calm working environment with clear classroom rules.

- Be specific and unambiguous when giving instructions.

- Make sure instructions are understood, especially when using subject-specific vocabulary that can have another meaning in a different context.

AFASIC, 2nd Floor, 50–52 Great Sutton Street, London EC1V 0DJ
Tel: 0845 355 5577 (Helpline 11am–2pm)
Tel: 020 7490 9410 Fax: 020 7251 2834
Email: info@afasic.org.uk Website: http://www.afasic.org.uk

Sensory impairments

Hearing impairment (HI)

The term 'hearing impairment' is a generic term used to describe all hearing loss. The main types of loss are monaural, conductive, sensory and mixed loss. The degree of hearing loss is described as mild, moderate, severe or profound. Some children rely on lip reading, others will use hearing aids, and a small proportion will have British Sign Language (BSL) as their primary means of communication.

How can the subject teacher help?

- Check the degree of loss the pupil has.
- Check the best seating position (e.g. away from the hum of OHP or computers, with good ear to speaker).
- Check that the pupil can see your face for facial expressions and lip reading.
- Provide a list of vocabulary, context and visual clues especially for new subjects.
- During class discussion allow only one pupil to speak at a time and indicate where the speaker is.
- Check that any aids are working and whether there is any other specialist equipment available.
- Make sure the light falls on your face and lips. Do not stand with your back to a window.
- If you use interactive whiteboards, ensure that the beam does not prevent the pupil from seeing your face.
- Ban small talk.

Royal National Institute for Deaf People (RNID), 19–23 Featherstone Street, London EC1Y 8SL Tel: 0808 808 0123 (Freephone helpline)
British Deaf Association (BDA), 1–3 Worship Street, London EC2A 2AB
British Association of Teachers of the Deaf (BATOD), The Orchard, Leven, North Humberside HU17 5QA
Website: www.batod.org.uk

Visual impairment (VI)

Visual impairment refers to a range of difficulties, including those experienced by pupils with monocular vision (vision in one eye), those who are partially sighted and those who are blind. Pupils with visual impairment cover the whole ability range and some pupils may have other SEN.

How can the subject teacher help?

- Find out the degree of sight impairment.

- Check the optimum position for the pupil, e.g. for a monocular pupil their good eye should be towards the action.

- Always provide the pupil with their own copy of the text.

- Provide enlarged print copies of written text.

- Check use of ICT (enlarged icons, talking text, teach keyboard skills).

- Do not stand with your back to the window as this creates a silhouette and makes it harder for the pupil to see you.

- Draw the pupil's attention to displays – which they may not notice.

- Make sure the floor is kept free of clutter.

- Tell the pupil if there is a change to the layout of a space.

- Ask if there is any specialist equipment available (enlarged print dictionaries, lights, talking scales).

Royal National Institute for the Blind, 105 Judd Street, London WC1H 9NE
Tel: 020 7388 1266 Fax: 020 7388 2034
Website: http://www.rnib.org.uk

Multi-sensory impairment

Pupils with multi-sensory impairment have a combination of visual and hearing difficulties. They may also have other disabilities that make their situation complex. A pupil with these difficulties is likely to have a high level of individual support.

How can the subject teacher help?

- The subject teacher will need to liaise with support staff to ascertain the appropriate provision within each subject.

- Consideration will need to be given to alternative means of communication.

- Be prepared to be flexible and to adapt tasks, targets and assessment procedures.

Severe learning difficulties (SLD)

This term covers a wide and varied group of pupils who have significant intellectual or cognitive impairments. Many have communication difficulties and/or sensory impairments in addition to more general cognitive impairments. They may also have difficulties in mobility, co-ordination and perception. Some pupils may use signs and symbols to support their communication and understanding. Their attainments may be within or below level 1 of the National Curriculum, or in the upper P scale range (P4–P8), for much of their school careers.

How can the subject teacher help?

- Liaise with parents.

- Arrange a work/subject buddy.

- Use visual supports: objects, pictures, symbols.

- Learn some signs relevant to the subject.

- Allow the pupil time to process information and formulate responses.

- Set differentiated tasks linked to the work of the rest of the class.

- Set achievable targets for each lesson or module of work.

- Accept different recording methods: drawings, audio or video recordings, photographs, etc.

- Give access to computers where appropriate.

- Give a series of short, varied activities within each lesson.

Profound and multiple learning difficulties (PMLD)

Pupils with profound and multiple learning difficulties (PMLD) have complex learning needs. In addition to very severe learning difficulties, pupils have other significant difficulties, such as physical disabilities, sensory impairments or severe medical conditions. Pupils with PMLD require a high level of adult support, both for their learning needs and for their personal care.

They are able to access the curriculum through sensory experiences and stimulation. Some pupils communicate by gesture, eye pointing or symbols, others by very simple language. Their attainments are likely to remain in the early P scale range (P1–P4) throughout their school careers (i.e. below level 1 of the National Curriculum). The P scales provide small, achievable steps to monitor progress. Some pupils will make no progress or may even regress because of associated medical conditions. For this group, experiences are as important as attainment.

How can the subject teacher help?

- Liaise with parents and TAs.

- Consider the classroom layout.

- Identify possible sensory experiences in your lessons.

- Use additional sensory supports: objects, pictures, fragrances, music, movements, food, etc.

- Take photographs to record experiences and responses.

- Set up a work/subject buddy rota for the class.

- Identify times when the pupil can work with groups.

MENCAP, 117–123 Golden Lane, London EC1Y 0RT
Tel: 020 7454 0454 Website: http://www.mencap.org.uk

SPECIFIC LEARNING DIFFICULTIES (SpLD)

The term 'specific learning difficulties' covers dyslexia, dyscalculia and dyspraxia.

Dyslexia

The term 'dyslexia' is used to describe a learning difficulty associated with words and it can affect a pupil's ability to read, write and/or spell. Research has shown that there is no one definitive definition of dyslexia or one identified cause, and it has a wide range of symptoms. Although found across a whole range of ability levels, the idea that dyslexia presents as a difficulty between expected outcomes and performance is widely held.

Main characteristics:

- The pupil may frequently lose their place while reading, make a lot of errors with the high frequency words, have difficulty reading names and have difficulty blending sounds and segmenting words. Reading requires a great deal of effort and concentration.

- The pupils' work may seem messy with crossing outs, similarly shaped letters may be confused, such as b/d/p/q, m/w, n/u, and letters in words may be jumbled, tired/tried. Spelling difficulties often persist into adult life and these pupils become reluctant writers.

How can the subject teacher help?

- Be aware of the type of difficulty and the pupil's strengths.

- Teach and allow the use of word processing, spell checkers and computer-aided learning packages.

- Provide word lists and photocopies of copying from the board.

- Consider alternative recording methods, e.g. pictures, plans, flow charts, mind maps.

- Allow extra time for tasks, including assessments and examinations.

The British Dyslexia Association
Tel: 0118 966 8271 Website: www.bda-dyslexia.org.uk
Dyslexia Institute
Tel: 07184 222300 Website: www.dyslexia-inst.org.uk

Dyscalculia

The term 'dyscalculia' is used to describe a difficulty in mathematics. This might be either a marked discrepancy between the pupil's developmental level and general ability on measures of specific mathematics ability or a total inability to abstract or consider concepts and numbers.

Main characteristics:

- *In number* the pupil may have difficulty counting by rote, writing or reading numbers, miss out or reverse numbers, have difficulty with mental mathematics, and be unable to remember concepts, rules and formulae.
- *In mathematics-based* concepts the pupil may have difficulty with money, telling the time, with directions, right and left, with sequencing events or may lose track of turns, e.g. in team games, dance.

How can the subject teacher help?

- Provide number/word/rule/formulae lists and photocopies of copying from the board.
- Make use of ICT and teach the use of calculators.
- Encourage the use of rough paper for working out.
- Plan the setting out of work with it well spaced on the page.
- Provide practical objects that are age appropriate to aid learning.
- Allow extra time for tasks including assessments and examinations.

Website: www.dyscalculia.co.uk

Dyspraxia

The term 'dyspraxia' is used to describe an immaturity with the way in which the brain processes information, resulting in messages not being properly transmitted.

Main characteristics:

- difficulty in co-ordinating movements, may appear awkward and clumsy
- difficulty with handwriting and drawing, throwing and catching
- difficulty following sequential events, e.g. multiple instructions
- may misinterpret situations, take things literally
- limited social skills which results in frustration and irritability
- some articulation difficulties

How can the subject teacher help?

- Be sensitive to the pupil's limitations in games and outdoor activities and plan tasks to enable success.
- Ask the pupil questions to check on understanding of instructions/tasks.
- Check seating position to encourage good presentation (both feet resting on the floor, desk at elbow height and, ideally, with a sloping surface to work on).

Speech, language and communication difficulties (SLCD)

Pupils with SLCD have problems understanding what others say and/or making others understand what they say. Speech and language difficulties are very common in young children but most problems are resolved during the primary years. Problems that persist beyond the transfer to secondary school will be more severe. Any problem affecting speech, language and communication will have a significant effect on a pupil's self-esteem, and personal and social relationships. The development of literacy skills is also likely to be affected. Even where pupils learn to decode, they may not understand what they have read. Sign language gives pupils an additional method of communication. Pupils with speech, language and communication difficulties cover the whole range of academic abilities.

Main characteristics:

- **Speech difficulties**
  Pupils who have difficulties with expressive language may experience problems in articulation and the production of speech sounds, or in co-ordinating the muscles that control speech. They may have a stammer or some other form of dysfluency.

- **Language/communication difficulties**
  Pupils with receptive language impairments have difficulty understanding the meaning of what others say. They may use words incorrectly with inappropriate grammatical patterns, have a reduced vocabulary, or find it hard to recall words and express ideas. Some pupils will also have difficulty using and understanding eye contact, facial expression, gesture and body language.

How can the subject teacher help?

- Talk to parents, speech therapist – and the pupil.
- Learn the most common signs for your subject.
- Use visual supports: objects, pictures, symbols.
- Use the pupil's name when addressing them.
- Give one instruction at a time, using short, simple sentences.
- Give time to respond before repeating a question.
- Make sure pupils understand what they have to do before starting a task.
- Pair with a work/subject buddy.
- Give access to a computer or other IT equipment appropriate to the subject.
- Give written homework instructions.

ICAN, 4 Dyer's Buildings, Holborn, London EC1N 2QP
Tel: 0845 225 4071
Email: info@ican.org.uk Website: http://www.ican.org.uk
AFASIC, 2nd Floor, 50–52 Great Sutton Street, London EC1V 0DJ
Tel: 0845 355 5577 (Helpline 11am–2pm) Tel: 020 7490 9410 Fax: 020 7251 2834
Email: info@afasic.org.uk Website: http://www.afasic.org.uk

Tourette's Syndrome (TS)

Tourette's Syndrome is a neurological disorder characterised by tics. Tics are involuntary rapid or sudden movements or sounds that are frequently repeated. There is a wide range of severity of the condition with some people having no need to seek medical help while others have a socially disabling condition. The tics can be suppressed for a short time but will be more noticeable when the pupil is anxious or excited.

Main characteristics:

- **Physical tics**
  These range from simple blinking or nodding through more complex movements to more extreme conditions such as echopraxia (imitating actions seen) or copropraxia (repeatedly making obscene gestures).

- **Vocal tics**
  Vocal tics may be as simple as throat clearing or coughing but can progress to be as extreme as echolalia (the repetition of what was last heard) or coprolalia (the repetition of obscene words).

TS itself causes no behavioural or educational problems but other, associated disorders such as Attention Deficit Hyperactivity Disorder (ADHD) or Obsessive Compulsive Disorder (OCD) may be present.

How can the subject teacher help?

- Establish a rapport with the pupil.

- Talk to the parents.

- Agree an 'escape route' signal should the tics become disruptive.

- Allow the pupil to sit at the back of the room to prevent staring.

- Give access to a computer to reduce handwriting.

- Make sure the pupil is not teased or bullied.

- Be alert for signs of anxiety or depression.

Tourette's Syndrome (UK) Association
PO Box 26149, Dunfermline, Fife KY12 7YU
Tel: 0845 458 1252 (Helpline) Tel: 01383 629600 (Admin) Fax: 01383 629609
Email: enquiries@tsa.org.uk Website: http://www.tsa.org.uk

The Inclusive Mathematics Classroom

Any system of education . . . that diminishes the school's role in nurturing its pupils' self-esteem fails at one of its primary functions.

(Bruner 1996)

Inclusion, empowerment and self-esteem

A positive self-esteem is an essential requirement for effective learning and if 'the project of inclusion is a political and social struggle to enable the valuing of difference and identity' (Corbett and Slee 2000), then our classrooms become the central stage for this process of valuing all pupils. We do this by valuing their contributions to the community – the classroom – that we manage.

An inclusive mathematics classroom must be centrally concerned with empowerment and the building of self-esteem in all pupils. The teacher in this classroom focuses on problem-solving activities and promotes a conjecturing atmosphere to enable all pupils to discuss and explore ideas.

Problem-solving

A problem-solving approach to learning where pupils are using and applying mathematics is an essential feature of an inclusive classroom. As Prestage and Perks (2001) suggest: '"Using and Applying Mathematics" should be integrated into the mathematics curriculum as much as possible. It is not an add-on: it describes a way of working mathematically.'

We can consider two aspects of the problem-solving classroom:

- The pupils are empowered and actively engaged in solving problems, together, independently or with support.

- The teacher (along with other professionals who share the classroom) is actively engaged in solving the problems of how children will learn through given objectives.

In order to develop all pupils' self-esteem, and for the group to engage fully in discussions about solving problems together, we must create a classroom climate for learning which encourages these features. John Mason (1988) argues that 'mathematical thinking is best supported by adopting a conjecturing attitude', and Greeno *et al.* (1997) assert that 'in constructing meaning in mathematics, we formulate and evaluate conjectures [and] build models'. The most effective classrooms are those where the children are engaged in constructing meaning in a 'mutually supportive' working environment. This doesn't happen by accident – co-operation can be taught; appreciating each other's contributions can be an explicit classroom value, and children can learn that allowing each other time to work things through is important for everyone. Children in these classrooms, therefore, carry a responsibility not only for their own learning, but also for everyone.

This is probably the greatest challenge we face in creating an inclusive classroom, often in school settings where the class has the most diversity in terms of achievement and social behaviour. However, if we create this atmosphere for learning, it also becomes our greatest ally.

McDermott (1993) suggests that: 'The question of who is learning what and how much is essentially a question of what conversations they are a part of'. If we accept this, and then consider these questions:

- Conversations with whom?

- About what?

- Using what vocabulary?

- For what purpose?

we begin to realise the impact of high expectations, of setting/streaming, of organising groups within our classrooms, of the vocabulary we choose to use in the lessons, of the activities we plan and the culture of our classrooms. This may appear to be an argument for mixed-ability teaching, but all class groups are diverse, however they are organised. Once we accept this premise, then our responsibility is to develop our range of teaching repertoires to enable *all* children to shine.

The inclusive mathematics classroom:

- empowers its pupils

- focuses on problem solving

- enjoys a conjecturing atmosphere, where discussion can flourish

This chapter attempts to address these issues through planning, and the following chapters look at teaching and evaluating mathematics lessons.

Views of mathematics: longer-term aims

How would your pupils respond to the question: What do you learn in mathematics lessons?

Children's answers invariably include examples of specific skills such as 'addition', 'times tables', 'angles', 'shapes', 'surveys', etc., but it is interesting to compare the responses of more able pupils with those who have difficulties with their mathematics. Often, the able pupil will tend to take a wider view of mathematics, and will identify processes such as 'proof', 'generalising' and 'being systematic', and then one or two might also suggest attitudes – 'not giving up', 'checking our work to see if we're on the right lines', 'trying to explore ideas', 'seeing the problem in a different way'.

Many of these responses can be seen as aspects of achievement in mathematics, as illustrated in the table below:

TABLE 4.1 ASPECTS OF MATHEMATICAL ACHIEVEMENT

Aspect of mathematical achievement	Example
Technical fluency – skills and knowledge	Times tables, methods for calculating, using measuring tools
Strategies for solving problems	Organising and tabulating data, generalising, explaining, proving, checking work
Attitudes to learning mathematics, including metacognition	Persistence, wanting to ask 'What if . . . ?', exploring ideas, checking how you are working

Answers in the second and third lines 'strategies for solving problems' and 'attitudes' rarely come from pupils who struggle with their mathematics. This analysis could highlight particular problems – either their own view of mathematics is limited, which could affect their learning, or they are only getting a diet of skills-based mathematics, without problem-solving contexts and without explicit experience of the attitudes to mathematics and to learning which are just as important. Their experience of mathematics is very likely to inform their view of it.

Many children with SEN do not only have to face their own difficulties, but low expectations too, whether their own, or from their wider social experience. However, low expectations may be expressed in a number of ways in school too: from insufficient challenge, which does not acknowledge a need to develop strategies and attitudes as well as skills, or sometimes from being in an environment where the most vulnerable learners are also placed together with pupils with the most challenging behaviours. There are a variety of strategies we can undertake to overcome these issues. Some are illustrated in the section on managing classroom behaviour later in this chapter, and others, such as effective questioning, promoting collaboration and the use of formative assessment, will be discussed in later chapters.

All children learn best when they are clear about what it is they should achieve. If children have a narrow view of what they should learn in mathematics lessons, then the wider views and attitudes need to be made explicit. We are interested in solving problems, and in order to solve problems, we have to know about strategies such as collaboration. We also have to demonstrate the fact that, although not all problems can be solved in five minutes, most can be solved with sustained effort.

Rogoff (1998) suggests that learning is a 'transformation of participation', and that a change in identity is the goal of learning. This can be likened to the distinction that we are teaching children to *become* mathematicians, rather than teaching them *about* mathematics. To participate in mathematical activities is to engage in the practices of, for instance, explaining, proving, generalising, being organised, hypothesising, reasoning and decision-making. None of these strategies evolve from doing pages of sums, or being taught a skill and then practising it, without discussing its application.

Being taught to become a mathematician allows children a:

sense of self, [which] in general, includes having various dispositions (habits of mind, predilections to view the world in particular ways), a certain kind of self-confidence and competence, and feelings of entitlement and empowerment. (Greeno *et al.* 1997)

Clearly, these considerations help us to clarify our longer-term aims for our children. This is an important distinction when we apply it to teaching children with SEN.

A vital aspect of being a mathematician is making decisions when solving problems. These decisions could be 'Which operation do I choose to solve this problem?' or 'How accurately do I need to measure this piece of wood?' or 'How should I present this information?' However, there is a common view that because children struggle with the *skills* involved in solving a problem, then the *decisions* about what skills to use, and when, and why, are assumed by the adults working with them, so that all that remains for the child is to make the calculations as instructed by the adult.

Here is a simple example. In an attempt to give children an experience in pie charts, a popular activity is to cut out a circle, and fold it into quarters or eighths, and then children ask either four people or eight people a question about, for example, favourite breakfasts, and they colour in one segment for each person, thus completing a pie chart of 'favourite breakfasts'.

So, what if there are 12 people in the class? What hypothesis has been addressed through this activity, which necessitated a pie chart in the first place? Indeed, have the children learned *how* to use pie charts, *when* to use them, and *why*? All these decisions have been taken away from the activity – worse, taken away from the children, who have become little more than actors for a series of tasks devoid of the real stuff of mathematics. This practice is disempowering, not perhaps intentionally, but perhaps because it is predicated on a belief that children must 'have the skills first' and then, at some later date, make sense of them. (Although this clearly will not happen in this classroom, since they have not been offered the *experience* of making sense of the skills.)

There also seems to be a huge pressure to 'get the task done' or to reach the answer by the end of the lesson, but it is the *process* of getting to the answer that is the stuff of learning. Making mistakes along the way, meeting and overcoming problems, persisting, checking and reviewing our work are what mathematicians do, and children can act like mathematicians at any level of ability. A two-year-old can generalise, and distinguish between cows and sheep in a field; the man who claims never to be any good at mathematics yet finds the middle of a room by using a stick and a piece of string (applying a sound understanding of symmetry) might not recognise his natural use of mathematics.

This is not to say that developing technical fluency is unimportant, for as Greeno *et al.* continue: 'In constructing meaning in mathematics, we formulate and evaluate conjectures [and] build models. . . . [For this] we must have the relevant mathematical tools at our disposal.'

The view that children should not be exposed to problem-solving until the skills are 'secure' means that they could then be presented with a diet of counting to 20 for years, with little room for other aspects of mathematics.

Expectations, progression, understanding

An understanding of inclusion also highlights expectations – of all those concerned with the children's learning, including the children themselves. As one of the four key principles underpinning the National Strategy (DfES 2001), it should change our discourse about children with SEN from 'they can't do this' to 'they will have difficulties in achieving this, and so I need to plan to address these difficulties'.

For example, there are parents, pupils and professionals who claim that 'children with SEN can't do algebra', suggesting a deep misunderstanding of algebra *and what it is for*. DfES (0292/2002) *Accessing the National Curriculum for Mathematics* offers examples of what pupils with special educational needs should be able to do at each P level. It gives, for example, at level P2 in algebra:

Start to associate particular routines with significant events – for example, when particular people arrive it will be time for dinner.

Here, algebra is understood to be concerned with relationships, understanding links and connections, and our expectation is that this understanding is an important entitlement for all pupils.

Children's expectations also have an impact on their own learning. Mason (1988) states:

The pressure of new work is always present when studying mathematics, and it is compounded by the pressure, mounting to hopelessness and panic, of previous work only partly comprehended and insecure.

We can plan for accurate assessment (Chapter 6) and careful progression to help overcome this panic, but we should above all be planning for *understanding*.

There are some who may argue that we could give children a method that works, and they may come to understand it later.

Consider the example of multiplying numbers by ten, e.g.:

- $10 \times 2 = 20$

- $10 \times 9 = 90$

- $10 \times 16 = 160$

Many children make sense of this experience by suggesting that we add a nought. Many children take this view into adult life. Many teachers, assistants or other adults use it to help children see the pattern, and therefore multiplying by ten is down to adding nought. It's a method that works, but only in a limited context . . . What understanding of the process of multiplying by ten is happening here?

Consider these:

- $10 \times 2 = 20$

- $10 \times 2.5 = ?$

- $10 \times 3 = 30$

Many children answer $10 \times 2.5 = 2.50$, because they are doing just as they have been told. They add a zero. Some get further confused, and offer $10 \times 2.5 = 20.5$, perhaps using the result $10 \times 2 = 20$, and realising that the answer ought to be bigger.

In teaching children a trick, like adding nought for multiplying by ten, we disempower them – keep them at a distance from genuine understanding of the number system and how it works. We fall into this trap perhaps from pressure of time and coverage, or perhaps because we see that it is difficult for some to understand and that completing the questions correctly has become the goal of the lesson rather than learning how to think mathematically.

Progression

For this reason, it is important to consider progression in developing children's understanding of mathematical ideas very carefully. The National Strategy Frameworks for Primary (DfES 1999) and for Key Stage 3 (DfES 2001) and the DfES 0292/2002 document described above can be used together for this purpose. The progression of objectives is clearly identified for each year group, and for children with SEN working at the P levels. The large task is to put them together to illustrate a clear line of progression for each set of mathematical objectives. An example is given in Table 4.2.

TABLE 4.2 IDENTIFYING PROGRESSION IN HANDLING DATA AT KEY STAGE 3, FROM P1 TO ABLE YEAR 9

P level Year	Objectives
P1	Show emerging awareness of activities and experiences. May have periods when they appear alert and ready to focus their attention on certain people, events, objects or parts of objects. May give intermittent reactions, e.g. show interest as groups of items are touched on the face or moved down their arm towards their hand, where they grasp as items enter the palm.
P2	Begin to be proactive in their interactions. Communicate consistent preferences and affective responses. Recognise familiar people, events and objects. Perform actions, often by trial and improvement, and remember learned responses over short periods of time. Co-operate with shared exploration and supported participation, e.g. be proactive in instigating events, reaching out and expressing preferences for objects and actions, and enjoy repeated events.
P3	Use emerging conventional communication. Greet known people and may initiate interactions and activities. Remember learned responses over increasing periods of time and may anticipate known events. May respond to options and choices with actions or gestures. Actively explore objects and events for more extended periods. Apply potential solutions systematically to problems, e.g. begin to show awareness of representing one object using one photograph, perhaps using ICT.
P4	Show an interest in number activities and counting, e.g. may recognise written symbols and may use scribble or marks to represent a count.
P5	Demonstrate an awareness of contrasting quantities by making groups of objects with help, e.g. begin to indicate/gesture towards pictures used in a simple tally system.
P6	Sort objects and materials according to given criteria, e.g. group pictures of everyday objects and say in which rooms in the house they may belong.
P7	Complete a range of classification activities using given criteria, e.g. sort a pile of coins by colour, size, shape or the name of the coin.
P8	Begin to use developing mathematical understanding and counting to solve simple problems, e.g. can select their favourite character in TV programme. Represent choices on a chart. Use chart to respond to questions such as, 'Which character does the whole class like best?'
Reception	Sort and match objects, pictures or children themselves, justifying the decisions made.
Year 1	Solve a given problem by sorting, classifying and organising information in simple ways, such as using objects or pictures, in a list or simple table. Discuss and explain results.

TABLE 4.2 *(continued)*

P level Year	Objectives
Year 2	Solve a given problem by sorting, classifying and organising information in simple ways, such as in a list or simple table, in a pictogram, in a block graph. Discuss and explain results.
Year 3	Solve a given problem by organising and interpreting numerical data in simple lists, tables and graphs.
Year 4	Solve a given problem by collecting, organising, representing and interpreting data in tables, charts and diagrams, including those generated by ICT, e.g. tally charts and frequency tables, pictograms, bar charts, Venn and Carroll diagrams.
Year 5	Solve problems by representing data in tables, charts, graphs and diagrams, e.g. bar-line charts, find the mode of a set of data.
Year 6	Solve a problem by representing, extracting and interpreting data in tables, graphs, charts and diagrams, e.g. line graphs. Find mode and range of a set of data, begin to find mean and median.
Year 7	Interpret diagrams and graphs (including pie charts), and draw conclusions based on the shape of graphs and simple statistics for a single distribution.
Year 8	Interpret tables, graphs and diagrams for both discrete and continuous data, and draw inferences that relate to the problem being discussed; relate summarised data to the questions being explored.
Year 9	Interpret graphs and diagrams and draw inferences to support or cast doubt on initial conjectures; have a basic understanding of correlation.
Year 9 able pupils	Analyse data to find patterns and exceptions, look for cause and effect and try to explain anomalies.

Sources: *Accessing the National Curriculum for Mathematics* (DfES (0292/2002)); *Framework for Teaching Mathematics: Reception to Year 6* (DfES 1999) and *Years 7, 8 and 9* (DfES 2001)

It is worth noting that this exercise not only clarifies the progression involved in learning some higher-order skills such as 'interpret graphs and diagrams and draw inferences', but also emphasises the links to all aspects of mathematics, e.g. in Year 2 'Use mathematical vocabulary to describe position, direction and movement' is an early stage in understanding angles (as a measurement of turning) and therefore in understanding how pie charts are constructed; in Year 4 'Know and use the relationships between familiar units of length, mass and capacity' is used in addressing the hypothesis 'tall people are heavier', for instance.

Through an activity designed to be problem-solving, children of all abilities therefore have opportunities to practise some of the skills relevant to their needs. More importantly, they are also working with a picture of how those particular skills are relevant and useful to the problem they are trying to solve. In trying to address the many different needs presented by a class of children, instead of 'individualised learning' that addresses the variety of learning objectives through several different contexts, a class could have one context that has multiple objectives. For example:

> Class 7B includes one child who has difficulties in counting, another needs practice in measuring accurately, others have difficulties in presenting their work, others may be poor at working collaboratively, some do not interpret diagrams and charts. The teacher devises a meaningful activity in data handling based on one of several different hypotheses, e.g. 'Boys have larger feet than girls' or 'Tall people have larger hands', which involves a range of objectives, including counting, measuring, drawing diagrams, working in a team, interpreting each others' charts, as well as many others which meet with the idea of a community of mathematicians working together, e.g. a group presenting its results to others, and trying to convince them that their data demonstrates that 'boys have bigger feet than girls', and justifying their choices in collecting certain types of data and presenting them in particular ways.

In this way, we do not start with the individual objectives at the level children appear to be working at, but instead look at the context from the higher-level objectives relevant to the year group, and then devise activities that will meet the range of objectives for the children.

Classroom culture

Let us consider the problems encountered in developing good mathematics teaching at the same time as creating an effective learning environment.

The Inclusion Statement from the National Curriculum Online (QCA) states that teachers should take specific action to respond to pupils' diverse needs by creating effective learning environments in which:

- The contribution of all pupils is valued.

- All pupils can feel secure and are able to contribute appropriately.

- Stereotypical views are challenged and pupils learn to appreciate and view positively differences in others, whether arising from race, gender, ability or disability.

- Pupils learn to take responsibility for their actions and behaviours both in school and in the wider community.

- All forms of bullying and harassment, including racial harassment, are challenged.

The Key Stage 3 National Strategy *Framework for Teaching Mathematics: Years 7, 8 and 9* states that where *teaching* is concerned, better standards of mathematics occur when:

- Regular oral and mental work develops and secures pupils' recall skills and mental strategies, and their visualisation, thinking and communication skills.

- There is whole-class discussion in which teachers question pupils effectively, give them time to think, expect them to demonstrate and explain their reasoning, and explore reasons for any wrong answers.

- Pupils are expected to use correct mathematical terms and notation and to talk about their insights rather than give single-word answers.

Clearly, the expectations are that for a significant part of the lessons we conduct thoughtful, reflective discussions about the mathematics problems we are solving. However, the problem many of us face is that we are often dealing with children whose difficulties are complex, and work against building a community of learners. Too common is the 'put-down' culture, where anyone successful is mocked, anyone who makes a public mistake is ridiculed, and some children cannot take turns or wait for others to answer, but they butt in and shout out. These attitudes inhibit learning in mathematics classrooms. It's not the answer we are working for – it is learning how to solve problems. That takes thinking, and thinking takes time.

Mason (1988) stresses that 'an attitude or atmosphere of conjecturing frees you from the dreadful fear of being wrong . . . we should bless our mistakes as golden opportunities.' Learning from mistakes is valid learning – as Mason continues: 'Being right lessens the opportunity to modify and learn.'

Sometimes, we are well intentioned by trying to reduce the scope for children with low self-esteem to make mistakes, and we modify problems so that they can succeed at each stage towards solving a problem, but we must be wary of taking all the decision-making out of problems.

Managing classroom behaviour

Effective management of classroom behaviour begins at the planning stage. If we are prepared for most of the possible and expected behaviours before we engage with the class, we can have a more balanced and calm view of the proceedings should they occur.

'A Conjecturing Atmosphere' (page 52) is a poster evolving from children discussing their rights and responsibilities in the classroom – with clear guidance from the teacher. We can plan to help them identify their fears of being wrong, and agree that the kind of classroom we want is one that allows everyone to learn. Used as a classroom poster or OHT, we can refer to the agreed principles throughout the year, reminding children that there are reasons why we want to work in this way.

A CONJECTURING ATMOSPHERE . . .

<u>What we want</u>
➢ An atmosphere where all pupils can learn effectively. This means that we have to learn together.
➢ A classroom where we can explain our own ideas and others will listen, and build on these ideas.

<u>Why we want it</u>
➢ Because everyone has the right to learn, and the teacher has the right to teach.
➢ Mutual respect builds the self-esteem of every individual.
➢ Because everyone is valued.

<u>How we make it happen</u>
➢ We talk as a group. We listen as a group. We share what we discover. We co-operate.
➢ We exchange meaning.
➢ We listen carefully to explanations and try to understand.
➢ We test conjectures, e.g. by finding counter-examples, or by helping each other to find a proof.
➢ We criticise constructively.
➢ Background noise is kept to a minimum, so that each person is able to think clearly.
➢ We keep focused on the task.

❖ Nobody ridicules.
❖ Nobody shouts.
❖ Nobody interrupts.

The rules are made to protect the rights and responsibilities for everyone in the classroom, including the teacher. Most behaviour is an aspect of culture – the vast majority of children will behave in ways they perceive is acceptable within the environment. Very few children will exhibit behaviours that will challenge the prevailing culture. So, most misbehaviour is low-level, minor disruption, but if this is left to go unchecked, then more extreme poor behaviour is more likely to occur, as it will emerge more easily from a general atmosphere of disorder.

Routines and expectations are important for establishing order, e.g.:

- clear expectations of what pupils should do at the beginning of the lesson – whether it is having books and equipment ready; waiting quietly behind chairs waiting to be seated or attempting an activity that is already written on the board;

- a clear signal for wishing to speak, e.g.: 'Thank you ladies and gentlemen' usually needs only saying no more than twice; one teacher moves a stool to the front of the classroom and takes a seat to establish calm and silence; another raises a hand to request calm.

Routines and expectations support the requirement of being consistent – both the day-to-day consistency for the individual teacher, and across the whole school. Meaning what we say and saying what we mean also reinforce this consistency, always carrying out actions that we say we will take.

Praise is also a valuable tool for establishing calm at the beginning of the lesson: those pupils who respond immediately to your request for silence can be thanked explicitly, even with the use of the school's reward system, and often this will calm a class down very quickly.

These points emphasise that effective management of behaviour stems from the quality of the relationships between teachers and pupils. There are ways in which these professional relationships can be enhanced. Teachers should consider:

- **Body position/language**
  Note carefully that speaking at eye level is less threatening than standing over a pupil.

- **Tone of voice/use of language**
  We must model proper conduct at all times.

- **Keeping calm**
  This is much easier when you have confidence in your own ways of establishing order in the classroom – hence planning for managing behaviour, and if necessary rehearsing your actions in response to behaviours you can predict. Confidence also arises from being sure of the consequences if poor behaviour should exceed that which is normally tolerated in the classroom.

- **Repair and rebuild**
  If things go wrong, it is important the child recognises that there is no grudge, and that there is a way back to the classroom where learning can take place again. It is best to try to ensure that you and the child can talk, calmly and quietly, away from the classroom, in preparation for the child's return to the next lesson.

If creating this climate for learning enables children to discuss their mathematical ideas freely, we are also allowing ourselves the chance to assess their understanding and to address their misconceptions more effectively.

Collaboration

To extend the opportunities for creating a mutually supportive (and therefore successful) classroom, we must also look at how groups or pairs of pupils can be helped to work collaboratively. There are sound educational reasons for collaborative working and joint problem-solving, and focusing how children handle the vocabulary of mathematics in their discussions. As Lave and Wenger (1991) point out, there is a difference between 'talking *about* a practice from outside and talking *within* it'.

The example of a lesson described in Chapter 6 and shown in Figure 6.3 illustrates a problem solved by pupils in pairs, where they are making decisions about what percentages of a quantity they wish to find, and learning about how their methods can be refined so that they can find any percentage of any quantity. This requires a rethink in the style of activity:

- open – 'find out whatever percentages you can', rather than closed – 'complete this set of pre-written questions';

- seating arrangements (for pair work, rather than individual work); and

- resources used (e.g. large paper, rather than individual books).

It also requires a change in view about what acceptable outcomes of a lesson look like – rather than a neat page of written work, children discuss solutions effectively or explain their own ideas. Sometimes this means nothing is written. There is no need for the teacher or pupil to feel guilty about that.

Collaborative pair working can also be a useful technique in whole-class discussions: if children have an opportunity to articulate some of their ideas to their partners, they have opportunities to refine their ideas, overcome mistakes, and use the vocabulary correctly before addressing the whole class. This is also a valuable point of intervention from other adults working in the class (see Chapter 7 – 'Managing Support').

MacGrath (1998) states that other advantages to facilitating co-operative relationships among pupils include:

- The greater the co-operation among pupils, the less conflict is likely between them.

- In an atmosphere of relative harmony, one potential source of anger that could be directed towards the teacher is eliminated.

- Pupils can help [and] more pupils can succeed and will have a greater investment in making school work for them.

It is important to plan the *purposes* of the collaborations taking place in the class. In classrooms where children can seem highly dependent on the teacher to overcome a range of difficulties (whether it is drawing a diagram, reading a piece of text or explaining the next step), planning for children to help each other can take the pressure off the teacher, and allows children to take responsibility for the success of the class. This point will be developed more fully in the section on differentiation in the next chapter, but, as McNamara and Moreton (1997) suggest:

In our view all children should have the opportunity to be a tutor and in particular, teachers should ensure that children with low self-esteem have the opportunity to be a tutor.

This means that the purposes need not just be restricted to facilitating access to learning (reading text for each other, making diagrams), but can be focused on the learning itself, e.g. explaining ideas to each other.

The physical environment, and resources for learning

Look at your room, and ask yourselves some questions, for instance:

- Is the wall display used to enhance learning?

- Is the equipment labelled to help children's independence?

- Does the seating help children to work collaboratively?

- Is furniture arranged so that wheelchair users can move around freely?

The physical environment can help us address some specific principles:

- Children need to be clear about the focus of the lesson – they need to know what they are learning, so that they can identify their own success – so the objectives of the lesson have a space at the front of the class.

- Demonstrations and instructions should be clear – accessible to all, and uncluttered.

- Children should learn to talk and must have a clear view of the vocabulary relevant to the lesson – therefore this vocabulary needs to be displayed, in such a way that it can be easily accessed.

- Children need opportunities to become independent mathematicians – they need easy access to materials and equipment, which they can then use to model, demonstrate and reason.

Pupils who use a wheelchair or other mobility aid will need a clear route to their desks and sufficient space to turn and manoeuvre in order to collect equipment. Pupils with physical disabilities should be involved in decisions about where they sit in the class. Consideration will also need to be given to the height and position of tables and chairs.

Some children with special educational needs may struggle with too much information, such as cluttered walls and cupboards, or with unclear writing on the board or on displays.

Appendices 4.3–4.8 illustrate some ideas for the use of the board and some posters.

The whiteboard or blackboard, OHPs, interactive whiteboards, computers and projectors (see Appendix 4.3)

You need a decent sized board, or one large and one or two small boards either side or on other walls, where the objectives and vocabulary of the lesson can be easily viewed and referred to. If you are lucky enough to have an interactive whiteboard – even better, but the overriding principle is that children learn better when they know where they are going (clear objectives) and have the tools (vocabulary) readily displayed. These are ongoing, updated displays, and should become a norm for each lesson.

There is debate about whether to use whiteboards because the glare from many light sources to be found in classrooms can be distracting to pupils. You will have specific information about any visual difficulties your children experience – some may react to bright light, others to low light, and some children may not benefit from enlarging texts or diagrams because their vision is concentrated onto one area. The IEP should show you this information; discussion with your SENCO would clarify any uncertainties. If glare is a concern, or if you have a blackboard anyway, you should still be prepared to have a screen readily available for occasional OHP use, perhaps considering reducing the glare with coloured transparencies.

Often, children with communication difficulties will need opportunities to express their understanding physically, and therefore to come out and demonstrate using diagrams, or move shapes about on the OHP. There are many useful tools for this, including OHT Cuisenaire rods, scales, e.g. OHT thermometer, clocks, graphs, shapes, that are straightforward to manipulate to aid demonstration. Different coloured acetates may be used for children who may read better with different background colours. With an interactive whiteboard, different coloured backgrounds can be easily dropped in.

Projectors linked to computers are also excellent sources of display. As with interactive whiteboards, the capacity to save information and the access to dynamic software (in geometry and graphical software especially) mean they are powerful tools for focusing children on the mathematics. Children's attention is enhanced, and the experience of whole-group discussion based on accurate and clear diagrams, charts and graphs reduces scope for misunderstandings.

As with all resources, we must decide if using ICT is the most appropriate medium for learning. The disadvantage of computers linked to projectors lies in the extent to which they inhibit your interaction with the class if you are stuck behind a computer. We should be actively teaching, and if we are, we need to point to things and demonstrate ideas, not just set off a slideshow. Interactive whiteboards enable you to move and emphasise, and children are often keen to use them too, to demonstrate their ideas and understanding.

The classroom number line (see Appendices 4.1 and 4.4)

This is essential. Blank number lines can be used for developing progression in understanding all four operations (see Chapter 5), and for comparing fractions, decimals and percentages; generating number sequences, and for the 0–1 scale in probability. As a visual tool for making calculations, it can be referred to regularly. It needs to be large enough to read clearly from any point in the classroom, and also to illustrate counting by large hand movements or walking from one number to the next.

Consider flexibility also here. Although a classroom number line with the numbers from −10 to 10 is shown as a way of helping children understand the relative sizes of negative numbers, and operations using negative numbers, it is also worth considering leaving the line blank, ready for any of the uses indicated above, and ready for a range of positions (e.g. from 20 to 40) or scales (e.g. from −100 to 100 or a scale involving decimals).

Vocabulary lists

The more children handle the vocabulary of mathematics, the more they become empowered as mathematicians. Subject-specific wordwalls are becoming increasingly common, but it is useful to review their purpose, and perhaps look at alternative ways of helping children focus on vocabulary.

It would be impossible to place the entire glossary of mathematical terms on a wall. Being selective, even the QCA glossary of KS3 mathematical terms is long. It's worth having for reference, because it is important to clarify meanings, but not perhaps worth having 'writ large' on the classroom wall – long lists of words can become sterile. Lesson or topic vocabulary lists, placed in an easy point of reference during discussions, however, enable you to focus children's attention on the language, its meanings and spellings (e.g. note discrete/discreet). You can then ask them to use the words to develop the quality of their explanations of their ideas, as you point to the words they could use. The vocabulary lists thus become a more dynamic learning aid.

Pupils' work

This is a way of explicitly valuing children's contributions. It only needs to be a few examples of work that clearly demonstrate what both you and the children feel are good pieces of work. With that in mind, it does not necessarily mean that the work has to look good, but it could give an opportunity for the children to annotate the work with an explanation of what they have found out. This process of explanation deepens their understanding.

Alternative recording methods

- photographs or videos of pupils engaged in practical tasks
- photographs of completed work using physical materials, e.g. Cuisenaire rods, shapes
- tape recordings of pupils' responses
- scribing
- dictaphone
- cut and stick methods for pupils who have difficulties with written tasks

Resources/mathematical equipment

Since some children with special educational needs have yet to master objectives usually related to younger children, we sometimes have a difficulty in finding resources and equipment that are relevant and meaningful to older age groups. The 'textbook for older children with SEN' doesn't – and perhaps shouldn't – exist. In any series of lessons written at a distance from the classroom, it is likely that the first one goes reasonably well, but the teacher will identify some issues from questioning the pupils which will prompt responsive planning for the next lesson. The more skilful the teacher in assessing pupils' understanding in the first lesson, the more responsive the second lesson should be, and the third, and so on. You can't write a textbook to do that, and with children with SEN, the cycle of plan, teach, learn, assess, evaluate, respond is even more critical to enable them to learn effectively.

An effectively resourced mathematics department will attempt to address the learning of the various mathematical topics (number, algebra, shape, data handling) through the range of learning styles (see Chapter 5). Appendix 4.9 offers a list of physical resources for a mathematics department – although it applies equally to an inclusive mathematics classroom. Berger *et al.* (2000) suggest we identify and use 'age neutral resources' and there are many useful resources listed here for effective teaching in mathematics, none of which look like a textbook. The range of resources allows us to develop a greater repertoire of teaching techniques.

Unfortunately, some people seem to believe in a hierarchy of knowledge that operates in a way that makes practical knowledge less valid than 'knowledge in the head'. No one learns to drive a car from reading instructions in a book and getting straight in to operate the clutch and gearshift immediately and brilliantly. Driving a car is a prized *practice*, but so are hypothesising, designing questionnaires and conducting surveys; reasoning, explaining and proving; constructing, modelling and evaluating. Using mathematical equipment allows children to engage in these practices with a visual and tactile stimulus.

For example, interlocking cubes can be used to generate sequences:

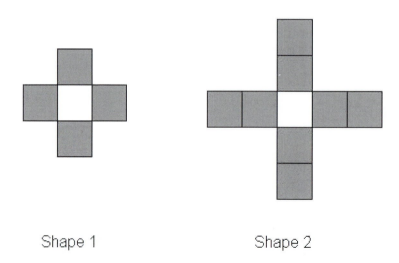

Figure 4.1 *Building a sequence of shapes using interlocking cubes*

The following instructions and questions develop the lesson:

- *Build the third shape.*
- How many grey cubes?
- How many white cubes?
- How many cubes altogether?
- What about the fourth shape? How do you know?
- The tenth shape? How do you know?
- The hundredth shape? How do you know?
- *Create a table of results* (see Table 4.3 below).
- Is there a pattern in the numbers?
- Is there a way of working out how many there are in the hundredth shape without counting?
- Why do we put the results in order?
- *Extend the table of results, to include larger numbers* (see Table 4.3).
- What about the twentieth shape?
- The millionth? How do we write this?
- How does this help us write an expression for the number of cubes in the nth shape?
- Is there always one white cube?

TABLE 4.3 CREATING A TABLE OF RESULTS FROM A SEQUENCE OF SHAPES

Shape Number	Number of White Cubes	Number of Grey Cubes	Total Number of Cubes
1	1	4	5
2	1	8	
3			
4			
5			
10			
20			
m			
n			

At a million, we know that each arm has one million grey cubes, so there are four million grey cubes + 1 white cube altogether. This can be written as 4m+1 for short here (a beautiful, natural use of algebra). M for million, or n for any, gets children into the *practice* of representing sequences algebraically . . . for it is a practice, just like driving. Further, children can see the physical development of a sequence and explain why their rule is four times the shape number plus one (because there are four arms and one in the middle). This gives them an opportunity to reason.

The same cubes can be used to build shapes, exploring relationships between volume and surface area, and so on. However, the mathematical equipment is sterile without appropriate questions to stimulate thinking.

For instance, if we build a cuboid with dimensions $2 \times 3 \times 4$, would we need twice as many cubes if we doubled the dimensions?

This is just one example of using equipment to develop mathematical thinking. It is beyond the scope of this book to examine the use of all the equipment listed – but examples of some of the questions are given below.

Cuisenaire rods

Cuisenaire rods can be used to form 'factor walls' or 'fraction walls' (Figure 4.2 below). Some of the questions that emerge could be:

- How many red rods make the same length as the orange?

- Does the light green rod fit exactly into the orange? Why not?

- Are there other rods that fit exactly into the orange?

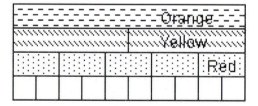

Figure 4.2 *Building a Cuisenaire fraction wall*

A Cuisenaire factor wall can easily become a fraction wall if we talk about 10 whites = 1 orange, so 1 white is $\frac{1}{10}$ of an orange rod, and so on.

Figure 4.3 *Demonstrating that 3 is not a factor of 10*

Figure 4.3 demonstrates that although 3 is not a factor of 10, it is still a fraction of it $\left(\frac{3}{10}\right)$.

Labelling

It is important to consider labelling all the equipment clearly to enable children to become independent and spontaneous users of it. To demonstrate an idea, we often need to model a situation using equipment. For example, in showing that if $4 + 6 = 10$, so $6 + 4 = 10$ (demonstrating the commutative law of addition), we could use Cuisenaire rods again (Figure 4.4).

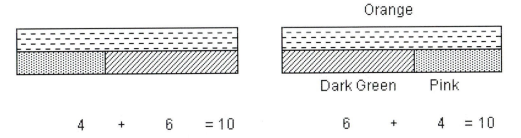

Figure 4.4 *Modelling mathematical ideas – the commutative law of addition, illustrated using Cuisenaire rods*

Ideally we would want children to learn to demonstrate rules in these ways. Feeling free to use equipment is a small step towards this.

Displays, posters

Appendices 4.4–4.8 illustrate possibilities for the classroom walls, if you are lucky enough to have any to work with. It is highly unlikely you have four walls – one is bound to be a bank of windows but the ideas are there to adapt.

100 squares (Appendix 4.8)

There are many commercially manufactured 100 squares, with ideas for activities. Consider some 100 squares that start with 1 at the bottom (Appendix 4.8), to aid the language of 'going up in tens', 'getting larger', etc.

Times table charts (Appendices 4.6 and 4.7)

This is a useful idea from *Education Initiatives* (2001) (see sources list, Appendix 4.14). As an excellent aid to help understand the links between the tables, these can be used as frequent lesson starters to rehearse table skills and explore the links in the number system.

The handling data cycle

The diagram shown in Figure 4.5 (page 62) is useful in a number of ways:

- To help children identify where they are in solving a problem – so that they know what they might need to do next, or so that they can understand where their current work fits into the whole picture. So, for example, if children have collected their data, they can be guided towards processing (making calculations) or representing their data (choosing the right charts, graphs or diagrams).

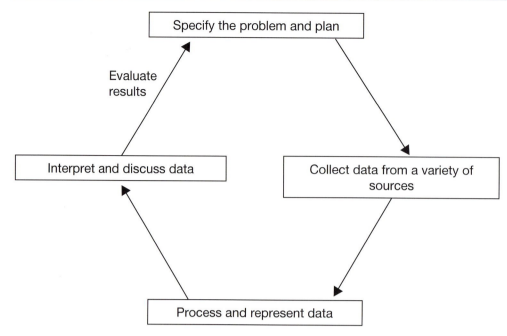

Figure 4.5 The data handling cycle, Key Stage 3 National Strategy, *Framework for Teaching Mathematics: Years 7, 8 and 9,* page 18 (DfES 2001)

- To help children evaluate how they are working. For example, if children have interpreted data, but find that their conclusions cannot say anything about their original hypothesis, they need to go back to their original plans and address how they designed their questionnaires, or review the decision they made on what data to collect.

- The cycle illustrates to teachers that each phase has a place in the overall context, e.g. teaching children *about* graphs and bar charts, by giving them lots of practice in drawing them for different situations, is not the same as teaching children how to use them, and why, and these aspects must be explicitly taught.

- As a planning tool, teachers can identify which parts of the cycle children need to practise further. If children are weak in interpreting their results, this might highlight a need for plenty of discussion based on a range of graphs, charts and diagrams.

Mathematical papers

The wide variety of mathematical papers provides a range of opportunities for different mathematical activities. Some very large centimetre squared paper is useful, especially for drawing fractions of a number line, where the line is 60 cm long. This is a good number because it has many factors, and many fractions of it can be found. Other papers bring in other mathematical ideas – isometric dotty is useful for translating 3D images onto 2D paper, and children can count the dots to help them draw shapes with the correct dimensions. Appendix 4.10 shows examples of some activities based on different types of dotty paper (Appendices 4.11–4.13).

Wider considerations in planning

Many teachers are concerned that lessons have to reflect other wider issues, such as literacy or citizenship. A brief examination of the style of teaching and learning that has been planned should indicate that such issues become a normal part of the lessons. There is no additional planning for literacy, because we are planning for 'mathematical literacy' in the ways we promote handling vocabulary, and children discussing, reasoning, explaining, etc. Our writing has a specific mathematical purpose.

For some children with SEN, a writing frame provides an effective structure to their thinking. Appendix 4.15 offers a possible example for structuring a data-handling project. Work in handling data has much to do with convincing others of interpretations of data. This can be expressed orally or in writing, and then presented to the whole group. Formal presentations of findings from statistical surveys can lead to children justifying their results, and the class engaging in joint evaluation of the findings.

Again, this relies on a conjecturing atmosphere, where it is safe for pupils to have their work analysed publicly, but their literacy skills are developed in an activity that has authenticity and, therefore, credibility. Mathematical literacy is not developed through word searches, but through this kind of meaningful activity.

We could use a similar example to illustrate how we are developing children's experience of citizenship. We become citizens through experiencing our society's practices and reflecting on these experiences. In the example given above, a classroom is described which can be likened to a community of young mathematicians, who may generate hypotheses, identify the information they require to convince others that their hypotheses are correct (or not), present this information in ways to illustrate their arguments, and then justify their results and methods. Other pupils can then explain why or why they are not convinced, and try to formulate appropriate questions. This is one example of modelling how we can operate as effective citizens. Planning these lessons takes into account how the class will collaborate, as well as the mathematics the children will learn.

Inclusive classrooms therefore address the entitlement of all pupils to all aspects of learning, and each of these aspects is seen as an integral part of the activities of the classroom.

Appendix 4.2 shows an example of a basic planning sheet, which will be developed throughout the course of the book. Later chapters will look at how to plan for differentiation, assessment and planning for other colleagues in the classroom.

Planning for misconceptions

Even before we teach, it is worth evaluating the planning by at least asking the questions:

- What difficulties will the children have with understanding this (or these) objective(s)?

- How can I prepare to meet these difficulties?

Then you can look at the range of resources (see Appendix 4.9), ideas, equipment, staffing and the collaboration with other pupils as possible solutions to this problem – and you can see the need to plan to use these solutions.

The examples that follow are based on objectives from the Key Stage 3 National Strategy *Framework for Teaching Mathematics: Years 7, 8 and 9* (DfES 2001). These objectives are listed in Year 7.

Objective: **Recognise vertically opposite angles**
Possible difficulties – Children may think that the angles have to stand vertically, instead of realising that the angles are vertically opposite however the diagram is rotated; children may not understand which angles are 'opposite'.
Possible solutions – Use colours, as well as conventional notation to indicate the angles that are vertically opposite; use OHT of two crossing lines – rotate it and clarify that the angles are still vertically opposite. Check their understanding of 'opposite' with simple activities in the classroom.

Objective: **Recognise the first few triangular numbers, squares of numbers to at least 12 × 12 and the corresponding roots**
Possible difficulties – Children may not relate the term 'square numbers' to the shape of a square, and therefore have no idea that the root of the square's area is equivalent to the length of its side; they may not know how to generate the square or triangular numbers.
Possible solutions – Children make some squares – with interlocking cubes, diagrams, find a connection between sides and areas; using squared paper, what different sized squares can they make? What are the areas of these squares? Generate triangular numbers from realistic situations, e.g. How many red snooker balls are there on a normal sized snooker table? What if the table were smaller, and we had to use a smaller triangle? Larger? Explore with triangular diagrams.

Objective: **Explain and justify methods and conclusions**
Possible difficulties – Children may not be happy to do this in front of the class; they may not remember or know the correct vocabulary to use.
Possible solutions – Refer to vocabulary list; use TA to listen to children's explanations, helping them to clarify any points of misunderstanding, or to help them emphasise correct use of vocabulary – children may feel happier to address the whole class after speaking to the TA; child may wish to use OHT for presentation, or get help from a partner who does the presentation with the child's prompting.

A further example of support could be in the use of a speaking/writing prompt, where the language of the problem can be used as a guide. For example, if children were trying to solve the problem *Begin to make simple estimates* (numbers up to five, level P8), they might be asked to estimate how many adults would be able to sit on a bench seat (e.g. in a park or at a picnic table). The following lines could be used as a prompt to guide their thinking:

- *I think the answer is more than one because . . . ;*

- *In half the bench we would be able to fit in . . . adults;*

- *So in the whole bench we could fit in twice as many, which would make . . .*

For larger numbers, different situations could be used, e.g. estimating the number of buttons needed for a shirt:

- *The places we need buttons are . . . ;*

- *For these places we would need . . . buttons;*

- *Down the front we would need about . . . buttons to (a specified point, e.g. halfway)*

- *The total of these buttons is . . .*

Through clarifying the language children use, we can clarify their thinking. The writing frame offered in Appendix 4.15 is another example of this.

Summary

In planning an inclusive classroom, we must start with the question 'How do I empower all pupils to learn?' Through this question we can analyse the physical environment and the resources we use, the nature of the activities we plan for our lessons, the ways in which children work and the nature of the 'conversations they are a part of'.

The following chapters will examine how this looks in practice as we teach, and then how we assess both the children's understanding and our lessons' effectiveness.

Teaching and Learning Styles

Lesson structure and design

The design of our lessons reflects our beliefs about how children learn. If we believe that children doing pages of sums is an effective way of teaching children an understanding of mathematics, then our lessons would look like that most of the time. If we believe that there is far more than that to effective learning, we may prefer to see lessons where children can articulate their own understanding through guided use of mathematical vocabulary, either orally or through the drafting process in writing; where they experience mathematics through a variety of learning media, including physical activities and resources, visual imagery, and ICT; and where they are clear about the goals of their learning. Lessons reflecting the latter views will be designed with variety, based on a series of episodes, and will form part of a clearly planned scheme.

Structured mathematics lessons

The three-part lesson (Mental and oral starter/main activity/plenary; KS3 National Strategy: *Framework for Teaching Mathematics: Years 7, 8 and 9*, page 28, DfES 2001) offers a structure within which the values given above can be addressed. It is not necessary to adhere rigidly to three parts for the sake of it – some colleagues work to four or more parts, one of which is designed to set the context for the lesson itself, within the series of lessons that the children are experiencing at the time. Other colleagues regularly introduce mini-plenary sessions, where they engage in a questioning session to unpick some misconceptions they have uncovered during the main activities. The most important point is that an episodic, structured lesson offers us opportunities to use a variety of teaching styles, resources and ideas in order to address the different ways in which children learn. Designing lessons with this kind of structure enables us to be more effective, though we should not let it become a 'straightjacket'.

Oral and mental starters

These offer opportunities to address the following:

- developing and explaining mental calculation strategies;

- applying calculation skills in algebra;

- developing estimation skills;

- interpreting data (e.g. Appendix 5.1, an example of a graph designed to mislead, and another which through the use of lines falsely suggests a link between eye colour);

- visualising and describing shapes, movements and constructions (e.g. see sections on auditory, visual and kinaesthetic learning and on translating between these learning media);

- developing mathematical vocabulary;

- developing the ability to generalise, reason and prove.

    (KS3 National Strategy: *Framework for Teaching Mathematics: Years 7, 8 and 9*, page 29, DfES 2001)

None of these aspects should be considered as exclusively the domain of the starter – children explaining and discussing should be a feature of a large part of the whole lesson.

The example given later in the section on 'Questioning' illustrates the value of children explaining their own calculation strategies. We could also add to this list:

- the class sharing in joint problem-solving activities – because this may set the tone for the classroom culture we would wish to establish;

- dealing with misconceptions, to iron out some of the likely problems before children engage with the main activity.

Main activities and plenary sessions

Whereas the starter of the lesson could stand in isolation (because it could usefully provide practice in previously learned skills, or address an aspect of mathematics tackled some time ago or to be reviewed in the future), the main teaching and the plenary sessions are essentially more tightly linked. Indeed, it can be argued that plenary sessions are more successful when they emerge meaningfully from the activity that has been going on in the main part of the lesson. For example, the activity (Chapter 4) given with the green and white cubes/squares leads naturally to a question and answer session where the generalisations can be explored, even using symbols to represent the rules that we find. An extended plenary might explore different shapes, e.g.:

Shape 1, using triangles

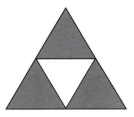

Can you make the next two shapes?
Create a table of results.

Shape number	White triangles	Grey triangles	Total number of triangles
1	1	3	4
2	1		
3			

How does using triangles change the sequence of numbers, from using squares?

Figure 5.1 *Developing a sequence of numbers from triangular shapes*

The plenary needs careful planning. It offers opportunities to draw together the learning from the lesson; allows pupils to reflect on their progress; allows teachers to assess children's learning and prepares both teacher and pupils for the following lesson. It is not effective just as a 'going through the answers' session, where no questioning about children's methods takes place – but the plenary offers an opportunity to use questioning effectively to assess understanding in different ways, e.g.:

- **using the rule**, e.g. 'Can you work out the number of cubes for the 100th shape?'

- **understanding how we solve the problem**, e.g. 'What patterns do you notice?' and 'Why do we put the numbers in a table?'

- **applying the rule**, e.g. 'If the total number of cubes used were 46, which shape have we made?'

Objective-led teaching

Where teaching is concerned, better standards of mathematics occur when lessons have clear objectives and are suitably paced.

(KS3 National Strategy: *Framework for Teaching Mathematics: Years 7, 8 and 9,* page 6

DfES 2001)

Setting clear objectives (and identifying learning outcomes) for your learners is an act of empowerment – it enables the pupils to identify what is expected of

them, and helps them to identify their own progress, which in turn develops their own capacity for independence. Black (1999) also highlights the importance of making explicit the goals of assessment – which will be explored more fully in the next chapter.

A difficulty to overcome is finding meaningful, mathematical learning activities that actually meet the objectives. To exemplify this, here is a Year 7 Key Objective:

Know and use the order of operations, including brackets.

This objective could be met in several ways, but it is worth examining the effectiveness of the various methods:

Method 1
State the rule: BODMAS/BIDMAS/(Brackets/Of, Indices/Divide/Multiply/Add/Subtract) and offer children a range of questions thus:

1 a) $4 + 8 - 2 =$　　　　b) $3 + 2 \times 5 =$　　　　c) $8 + 6 \times 2 =$

These questions are only related in terms of their level of difficulty, rather than being related in terms of enabling children to see trends or patterns in the results (as in Method 2).

Progression in this view of learning is therefore seen by introducing more complexity, e.g.:

2 a) $6(3 + 4) =$　　　　b) $2(1 + 9) =$　　　　c) $3(5 - 2) =$

Further questions could examine the presentation of division within a series of calculations, e.g.:

3 a) $\dfrac{16 + 2}{3}$　　　　b) $\dfrac{8 + 4}{4}$

Figure 5.2 *Addressing an objective through a method focused on the acquisition of skills*

Such a structure of progression focuses on acquisition of the various small skills – handling division, using brackets, etc. These skills are incorporated into the next activity, but it has an added dimension of enabling pupils to examine the purposes of the order of operations.

Method 2

We could offer children connected sequences of calculations, and invite them to identify rules and patterns in the results, e.g.:

Operations using brackets.
Multiplication and division.

Multiplication

1 a) $(2 \times 5) \times 3 =$ b) $2 \times (5 \times 3) =$

2 a) $(3 \times 5) \times 4 =$ b) $3 \times (5 \times 4) =$

3 a) $(4 \times 3) \times 3 =$ b) $4 \times (3 \times 3) =$

4 a) $(3 \times 5) \times 5 =$ b) $3(5 \times 5) =$

5 a) $(10 \times 3) \times 4 =$ b) $10(3 \times 4) =$

6 a) $(1 \times 2) \times 3 =$ b) $1(2 \times 3) =$

7 Write down what you notice with these multiplications. Why do you think this happens?

8) What are the volumes of these cuboids (all measurements are in cms)?

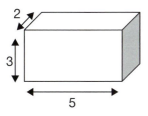
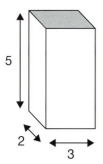

Divisions

1 a) $(12 \div 6) \div 2 =$ b) $12 \div (6 \div 2) =$

2 a) $(40 \div 10) \div 2 =$ b) $40 \div (10 \div 2) =$

3 a) $(36 \div 6) \div 3 =$ b) $36 \div (6 \div 3) =$

4 a) $(100 \div 10) \div 5 =$ b) $100 \div (10 \div 5) =$

5 a) $(24 \div 6) \div 2 =$ b) $24 \div (6 \div 2) =$

6 a) $(16 \div 2) \div 2 =$ b) $16 \div (2 \div 2) =$

7 Write down what you notice with the answers to these.

8) When do you need to use brackets

Figure 5.3 *Addressing the objective through a method that combines skills acquisition and an understanding of the purpose of the order of the operations*

Children could similarly explore addition and subtraction, and also examine the effect of mixed operations. Note this method uses the opportunity to link to another aspect of mathematics – volume of cuboids, to enhance understanding of both the order of operations and the calculation of volumes.

> **Method 3**
> We could gather some calculators together (that we know work in different ways, so will produce different answers) and attempt calculations with mixed operations and no brackets, and compare results. This should lead to a discussion about how we can achieve consistency with the results from all calculators, showing the need for brackets, and the need for a convention in the order of operations. Perhaps some of the calculations offered in Methods 1 and 2 above could be used for this.

Figure 5.4 *Addressing the objective through a problem to solve*

All these methods address the given objective:

[*Know and use the order of operations, including brackets.*]

- **Method 1**
  Could be argued as a direct (and possibly exclusive) teaching of the given objective. Although it may be argued that children are getting practice in calculations with the four operations, this is also true of all the examples.

- **Method 2**
  The issue is now placed within a problem-solving context, and further objectives come into play, e.g. *Present and interpret solutions in the context of the original problem; explain and justify (methods and) conclusions, orally and in writing. Use units of measurement to calculate and solve problems involving volume.*

- **Method 3**
  This example could introduce an objective in addition to example 2, such as *Carry out calculations with more than one step using brackets and the [calculator's] memory.*

In these examples, a greater range of mathematics emerges when we set the learning within the context of a problem for the class to solve. The second and third examples illustrate *why* we have an order of operations, whereas the first simply presents the rule as a convention for children to take on board. Some may argue that children must learn the skills before they can solve problems with them. However, given that the child who has difficulties with mathematics is likely to take longer on many activities, there is a danger that the wider understanding shown in examples 2 and 3 will be squeezed out if children experience activities where the goal of learning is only the acquisition of skills. It is therefore more likely that this child will experience a disjointed series of skills lessons, without sufficient exploration of their purpose – yet problem-solving is a fundamental aspect of the child's difficulty.

Teaching to a single objective is therefore not in itself a sufficient guarantee of a high-quality lesson – attention must be paid to a range of objectives, some of which entail using and applying mathematics.

Collaboration and differentiation

Problem-oriented activities emphasise not only agency (the capacity to initiate, explore, complete and evaluate activities, Bruner 1996) but also collaboration. Rogoff (1998), discussing Vygotsky's theory, argues that 'the model of most effective social interaction is joint problem-solving with guidance by a person who is more skilled.' In many classrooms, the nature of discussion is often one of children 'reporting' their findings from an activity, and less of children solving problems together through talk. In order to learn *to* talk, rather than *from* talk (Lave and Wenger 1991), we must provide occasions in which the real stuff matters so much that students engage in literacy 'as a part of conducting their everyday work in classrooms' (Greeno *et al.* 1997).

The examples given above of setting the mathematics within a problem-solving context enable the teacher to construct paired or group work so that children's findings can be discussed, and their reasoning shared.

McNamara and Moreton (1997) describe a 'model for differentiation', where talk and collaboration are the key features. They state that the rationale for collaboration is that it helps learners to:

- develop their own thinking through talk (by handling the vocabulary through which they think and reason (Bruner 1996));

- get support – to get help in their thought and language development and the emotional support which helps their sense of self-worth and self-belief;

- value their achievements – through collaboration children can be helped to ascribe specific roles and therefore feel a clear sense of responsibility when they are successful in their task.

In pairing or grouping children, this model cites Vygotsky's (1962) view that 'through explaining both partners in the pairing come to realise what it is they are thinking, clarify their thinking and understanding and sometimes come to new thoughts or concepts.'

Meeting differentiation through collaborative pairings addresses differences in learning styles, rather than considering differences in ability. So, for instance, if a child learns best through expressing ideas visually, they may be paired with another who reads and discusses ideas well, and together they can solve a geometric problem that is presented only in written form. Each person has a role to play in the partnership. Collaborative pairings can make meaning through any media – talk, diagrams, physical movements or using a range of mathematical resources for demonstration, but the planning required for this must also focus on the purposes of the collaboration (Murphy 1998).

McNamara and Moreton (1997) go on to argue that for paired activities there are two principles that should be taken into account:

- A joint product should result.

- Collaboration is a criterion for success.

Translating these principles to an activity, we could again refer to the three methods given above for understanding the order of operations. Children could for instance be grouped so that they explore the calculator problem (method 3) together. The joint product could be a report to the class on the effect of changing the order of the terms when using a calculator – for instance, comparing:

$$\text{a) } 2 \times 4 + 5 = \qquad \text{with b) } 5 + 4 \times 2 =$$

Part of their joint product could be to find other examples to explore and to check each other's calculations and to calculate using pencil and paper, as well as reporting on the effects for different calculators.

To illustrate how collaboration was a key for success, they could also report on the various roles taken by members of the group, how they supported each other when they came up with difficulties, and how successful they were at completing the work. This could be a time-budgeted part of the lesson.

There are too many benefits from this way of working for it to be ignored:

- it will evolve a mutually supportive classroom culture;
- children can work on their own targets with immediate support;
- responsibility for learning is firmly located with the child (teachers are responsible for the *management* of learning);
- problem-oriented activities can be used as the basis of the lesson.

It is also an expression of inclusion through valuing diversity, by using different learning styles in collaboration, and this clearly benefits learning.

Differentiation should also be addressed through effective, focused and planned questioning. Bloom's (1956) taxonomy is a useful tool to help plan questions that require different levels of thinking. This is explored more fully in the next section.

Questioning

The quality of questioning is a key feature of effective mathematics teaching. This can be analysed in a number of ways (e.g. by examining the questions themselves through constructs such as Bloom's taxonomy, or considering open and closed questioning (Framework, DfES 2001) or by examining their social impact, such as when to question, and how to manage it in class).

Both the quality of questioning and the impact of teachers' responses can be analysed through the following example:

> *Teacher:* 'Eight sevens?'
> Pupil A, holding out 10 digits says quietly to himself '70', then with 9 digits, '63' then with 8 digits he says '56' out loud.
> Not all pupils are paying attention.
> *Teacher – to next pupil:* 'Eight sixes?'
> Next pupil (B) is completely stuck.

The questions being asked of this class are closed, and the impression is that each pupil has to devise some quick way of answering without learning explicitly from each other. It is worth considering what kind of classroom culture would exist with this group in two years' time. Berger *et al.* (2000) emphasise the importance of giving children time to respond. A feature of many mathematics classrooms is the perceived norm of an automatic response to questions. The correct answer should not always be the aim of questioning – the working out and forming an explanation are more important goals, and these processes take time.

These waiting moments can also be used to praise a class for waiting, for not butting in, and teachers can model the patience, and reinforce the values that we are in a learning environment, and that we support people by allowing space and time to each other, not by giving the answers. This helps to build a mutually supportive and, therefore, successful classroom. Shouting out the answers stops children from undertaking the necessary thinking to get to the answer.

What learning could take place if the following happened instead?

> *Teacher:* 'Eight sevens?'
> *Pupil A:* (holding out 10 digits says quietly to himself '70', then with 9 digits, '63') then with 8 digits he says '56' out loud.
> *Teacher:* 'I like what you are doing here' (using praise). 'You're using a system' (explaining why the praise was due) – 'how did you work that out?'
> *Pupil:* 'I know that ten sevens are 70, so I counted two sevens back.'
> *Teacher to class:* 'Why did he count two sevens back?' and tries to model responses on the board . . .
> *Pupil:* 'He had ten sevens, but you asked for eight sevens, so you have to take two sevens away.'

Figure 5.5 models the pupil's calculation diagrammatically – building a visual image for the pupils. The number line is a powerful tool for this.

On the board:

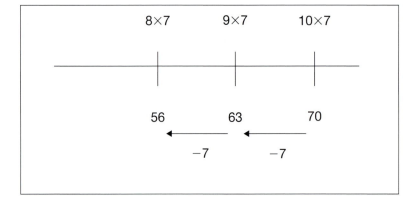

Figure 5.5 *Modelling a child's explanation, using a number line*

Now, turning to pupil B who claimed to be stuck, the response could be

Teacher: 'How could we use this method to calculate eight sixes?'
Pupil B might still claim to be stuck, but now there is some scaffolding on the board for understanding how the problem could be tackled.
Teacher: 'Could we use this work on the board to help us find the answer?'
There are several ways to use it, e.g.:

- repeat the model for 10×6 then 9×6 and then 8×6
- extend the above diagram to count back to 8×6

Or use other methods from other children, e.g.:

- 2×6, doubled and doubled again
- 8×3, doubled

Through comparison of children's methods, we are not only helping with the skills of multiplying, but giving greater insights into the workings of the number system, and showing that we value their methods by explicitly using them in other problems.

The kind of classroom culture that is being developed here is a genuine valuing of pupils' methods, thus building their self-esteem, but we are also evaluating a range of possible methods, finding which are effective and which could not always be applied, suggesting that that is what we do in mathematics classrooms. And we are not saying that pupils are on their own in their learning – solving the 8×6 could become a class problem to solve.

Such questioning also offers a greater number of opportunities to praise children, and as Hart (2000) states: 'A heightened sense of acknowledgement might be what persuades pupils to take whatever enhanced learning opportunities are introduced.' Praise is essential in building self-esteem and a positive classroom culture, and we can construct opportunities to use it meaningfully through our questioning – and this is a small but practical example of 'valuing diversity and difference' which underpins inclusion.

It is worth considering again what kind of classroom culture would exist in two years' time in a class where these kinds of interactions regularly took place.

Berger *et al.* (2000) offer this classification of questions:

- recalling facts

- applying facts

- hypothesising and predicting

- designing and comparing procedures

- interpreting

- applying reasoning

Children only experience 'recalling facts' when presented with a times table question, but the question 'How did you work that out?' immediately offers children the chance to design and compare procedures, and when this line of questioning is explored, they can go on to use reasoning and apply facts. Effective differentiation is therefore achieved through this type of questioning as it is specific and focused on the point of learning for each child. One question 'How did you work that out?' is relevant to the child who is able to use a method, but may need to explain it to be sure of it, whereas another question 'How could we use this method for an alternative problem?' requires the next child to recognise the applicability of a method they may not have considered before.

Using this classification, we can also analyse some written questions, and illuminate how different styles of questions allow children scope for wider learning opportunities. A classic GCSE Foundation paper question is given below.

What is the perimeter of this shape? (diagram not drawn to scale)

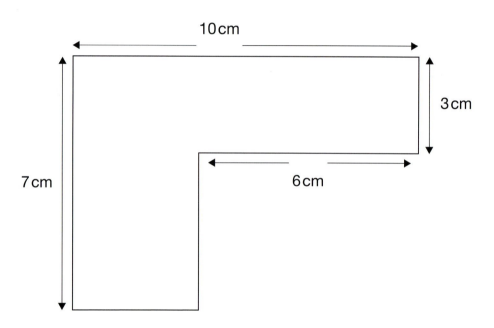

Figure 5.6a *GCSE style question on finding the perimeter of a shape*

Returning to the question at the beginning of Chapter 4 – 'What do we learn in mathematics lessons?' – we can examine what children learn from answering this question. Here, children are expected to interpret the problem and realise that they need further information – the remaining two lengths – so that they can add up six lengths to find the perimeter. Usually, if children don't understand the method, we can support them, but given this closed example, we are in danger of doing the whole thing for them. Nevertheless, the question invites children to apply reasoning to find the perimeter. However, as Prestage and Perks (2001) suggest, changing the question will change the mathematics that children experience. What happens when we remove some of the information?

What is the perimeter of this shape? (diagram not drawn to scale)

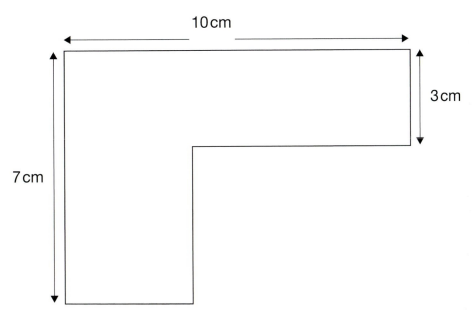

Figure 5.6b *Removing some information*

Here, children may be encouraged to ask 'What if . . . ?' such as 'What if the missing length were 8 cm or 5 cm, etc., and practise the style of the question. However, if they collected all their results, and were encouraged to say what they noticed, they might find that all the perimeters were the same. These simple techniques take children who have difficulties with their mathematics into discussing, reasoning, hypothesising and predicting (using Berger *et al.*'s classification), enabling them to make real sense of the mathematics they are encountering.

Finally, if we presented the problem with just the 7 cm and the 10 cm sides given, could the children still work out the perimeter? How do they work it out?

The mathematics takes another level of thinking, because it is now focused on the *concept* of perimeter, rather than focused on the *calculation* of it. This is a far deeper understanding than is enabled through the first question.

Changing the presentation of questions

Some basic sums could be presented thus:

$$
\begin{array}{cccc}
43 & 82 & 98 & 54 \\
+\ 28 & +\ 49 & +\ 14 & +\ 57
\end{array}
$$

Figure 5.7 *Standard presentation of sums*

The purpose of these is simply to practise a particular algorithm, namely to use column addition techniques, involving carrying tens (or hundreds). These sums do not necessarily help children understand the *concept* of addition, but they enable them to practise the *written technique* for solving them. If children do not understand what these presentations of addition mean, they need to look at number lines or physical objects (e.g. money, metre sticks, Diene's blocks or other place value tools) to help. They may also need to use these tools to help with the calculation.

Another issue with this presentation of the calculation is that it immediately guides children into one way of solving the problem – through the standard written algorithm. That's fine if that is the objective – but many of our children with SEN need to build their own mental strategies for calculating well before they engage with the written form.

If the first sum were presented horizontally, e.g. 43 + 28, what other strategies might we encourage? There are a few:

- the use of the number line (discussed in the section later in this chapter on visual imagery)

- the use of partitioning: 43 + 28 = (40 + 20) + (3 + 8) = 60 + 11 = 71

- compensation: 43 + 28 = 41 + 30 (by moving two from 43 to the 28) = 71

Alternatively, if the sum were presented in a more open way, we could encourage children to look for patterns. (A detailed look at the use of patterns is given later in this chapter.) By blotting out the 40, for example, we can have 10 sums.

$$■3 + 28 =$$

3 + 28; 13 + 28; and so on.

Here, we can encourage children to find what is the same, and what changes in each answer. This will give children an opportunity to learn a self-checking mechanism – that every time an 8 and 3 are added in the units, a one will result in the units column. The use of pattern is a powerful tool in checking accuracy. It will also give a greater insight into place value, by analysing the effect of changing the value in the tens column.

Children who experience difficulties in mathematics need to have these points made explicit, to clarify their understanding. To do this, children must discuss their own findings and ideas – to create their own understanding 'instead of rehearsing or recreating knowledge produced by others' (Wiske 1998).

Appendix 5.2 looks at some mathematical questioning through Bloom's taxonomy. However, this taxonomy should not be considered as a hierarchy of increasing exclusivity. For instance, all children could have the chance to:

- look at poorly drawn graphs and say what might be wrong with them (Appendix 5.1)

- predict later numbers in a sequence

- analyse results from a statistical survey.

All pupils are entitled to deal with the higher levels of questioning that this taxonomy helps us to identify.

Learning styles

A teacher for the inclusive classroom must recognise that restricting learning opportunities to one favoured style of presenting ideas – presentations both by the teacher and by the children – will disadvantage many pupils in the class. The development of research in preferred learning styles has raised our awareness of the need to consider a range of learning activities not just for the sake of children's access and expression but also because it is clear that the mathematical content – and thus what can be learned from the activities – takes on different qualities when using different media.

Take, for example, a problem from Ollerton (2003) (page 16 – 'Wholesome triangles'):

● How many different triangles can be made with a perimeter of 30 cm so that all sides are of whole number length?

This can be presented to children in a number of ways.

Restricting children to writing down their answers as numbers may mean that they fall into the trap of thinking they are only looking for sets of three whole numbers that sum to 30, e.g. 1, 1, 28; 1, 2, 27; 2, 2, 26, etc., without realising that these initial solutions could not possibly make a triangle. They have therefore interpreted the problem as a 'sum to 30' exercise, instead of a 'three possible sides of a triangle' problem.

Some children, even with the aid of diagrams, may still fall into this trap, because there is no 'real' or physical experience underpinning their presentation of results.

For some children, it is only when using sticks or string cut to appropriate whole-number lengths that they will recognise *both* conditions of the problem – that the perimeter is 30 cm *and* that the three sides have to fit together to form a triangle.

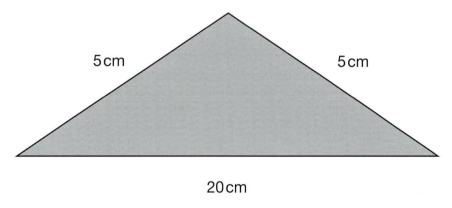

Figure 5.8 A 'problem' triangle!

This should be viewed as a learning activity, not an assessment task, but even then we should ask why an assessment task should be restricted to the written number form. As a learning activity, children are provided with a greater insight into the relationship between the sides of a triangle when they have something physical to manipulate.

For some people, using physical resources represents a lower order of mathematical understanding, for use only with younger children and those who experience difficulties. For others, there may be concerns that presenting ideas physically or using diagrams slows down the pace of lessons, and that there is enough pressure to 'cover' the curriculum as it is.

If our first principle is to create an inclusive classroom, then we must be concerned about building the self-esteem of pupils, and we must ensure that we meet their rights to understand the ideas we are teaching, and we therefore use the range of techniques necessary to achieve this. Children are entitled to the self-esteem that arises from understanding, and any means to achieve that – physical (including tactile), visual or auditory – should be explored.

Some of the ways we could meet the needs of the different learning styles in the mathematics classroom are illustrated in the table below:

TABLE 5.1 EXAMPLES OF WAYS TO MEET THE NEEDS OF PUPILS WITH DIFFERENT LEARNING STYLES

Learning style	Support learning through
Visual	Wall displays, posters, flash cards, graphic organisers, graphs, charts, number lines, spider diagrams, videos, concept maps, colour highlighting (e.g. colour angles which are the same in diagrams).
Auditory	Use audiotapes and videos, storytelling, chants. Allow learners to work in pairs and small groups regularly. Discussion, stories. Collaborative writing – presentations for the class. Talking about the vocabulary, e.g. explaining the term 'percentage' and its roots in 'cent – 100' and other real-life uses of the root 'cent' – century. Mental starters – visualisations.
Kinaesthetic	Use physical activities, competitions, board games, role-plays, whiteboards, movement (e.g. illustrating that angle is a measurement of turn, experiencing rotations), card-sorting. Use a range of mathematical equipment, e.g. interlocking cubes, rods, geometrical strips, Taktiles (Algebra through Geometry pack (G. Giles)), probability experiments. Intersperse activities that require students to sit quietly with activities that allow them to move around and be active.

It is worth exploring in a little detail how some of the techniques for teaching to meet the learning preferences can enhance understanding in different ways. Preferred learning styles do not exclude access to learning via other methods – visual learners *can* listen, all learners can benefit from understanding a mathematical situation physically, and learners can express themselves through the whole range of learning media.

Visual learners, visual imagery

The number line (Appendices 4.1, 4.3 and 4.4) was introduced in Chapter 4. It is worth briefly demonstrating its power, both as a visual aid and as a way of identifying progression in learning calculating techniques with all four operations – addition, subtraction, multiplication and division.

Firstly, the blank number line may be presented in different forms, depending on the level of support you wish to offer the child:

Marked and labelled

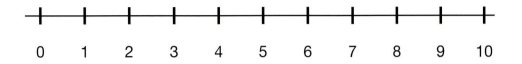

Marked and unlabelled

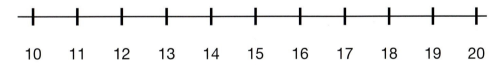

Empty number line

_____

Focusing on different sections of the number line

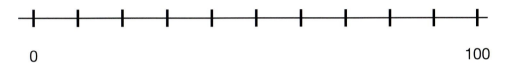

Figure 5.9 *Different types of number line (Source: Progression from Mental to Calculator Skills, DfES 0046/2004)*

Some examples of how these lines may be used with all four number operations are illustrated below.

Addition

Addition can be seen as *counting on,* using each integer as a step, or by using larger jumps, say in fives or tens, when children become more comfortable with counting in this way. The steps can be used to illustrate the mental processes that children employ, for example:

$$4 + 12 = 16$$

Children may calculate this as 4 + 2 + 10 (Figure 5.10a), or 4 + 10 + 2 (Figure 5.10b) or 4 + 6 + 6 = 10 + 6 = 16 (Figure 5.10c).

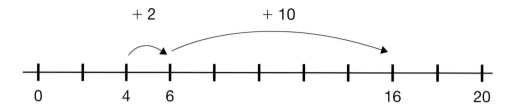

Figure 5.10a 4 + 12 = 4 + 2 + 10 = 16

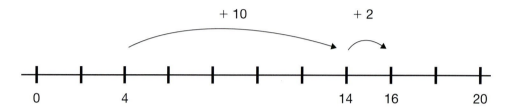

Figure 5.10b 4 + 12 = 4 + 10 + 2 = 16

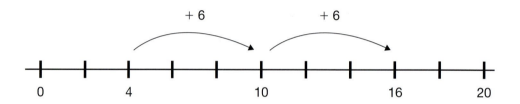

Figure 5.10c 4 + 12 = 4 + 6 + 6 = 10 + 6 = 16

Illustrating children's different methods visually allows others to compare their own methods, and offers different insights into the number system. Using the last example highlights the value of complements to ten as a mental addition technique; the first two show that when adding ten, the unit value does not change.

The technique can be extended to handling decimals, and indeed this reinforces the understanding of the patterns and similarities throughout the number system, e.g.:

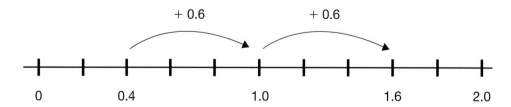

Figure 5.10d 0.4 + 1.2 = 0.4 + 0.6 + 0.6 = 1.0 + 0.6 = 1.6

Subtraction

Subtraction using the number line builds on these ideas of using counting on. It's a bit like a visual form of giving change by counting to useful whole numbers of tens or hundreds.

Teaching children about the 'mechanics' of subtraction has long been separated from establishing an understanding of subtraction. By setting out subtraction calculations in columns, and devising ingenious methods for dealing with 'borrowing' or 'paying back', we fail to address an understanding of difference. In contrast, looking at the calculation using a number line, or working out how much change to give, involves communication and checking which aids understanding. Teaching children the column method does not help them understand the *concept* of differences or of subtraction: it teaches only about the method. Further, there is little scope for progression in teaching column subtraction, because it has to be significantly modified in the type of situation given below. When the method goes wrong, however, the children have little recourse to understanding why, and do not – or cannot – check their work.

For example:

$$
\begin{array}{r}
105 \\
-68 \\
\hline
163
\end{array}
$$

Figure 5.11 *A common subtraction error*

The answer is meaningless, but this happens often, because children are using a method they do not understand, to work on a concept they don't understand. In this case, the child has taken the 5 from the 8, and the zero tens from the 60. It's much easier to deal with than taking the 8 from the 5, and the 60 from zero.

If we taught for understanding through progression and by developing visual imagery through the number line, children would have a chance of seeing whether their answers made sense or not. This would not cure everything, but it would give children a way of 'seeing' the subtraction, and help to give a feel for the validity of their answers. It relies on children knowing complements to ten (and multiples of ten), complements to 100 (in tens), and then adding two single digit numbers to a multiple of ten.

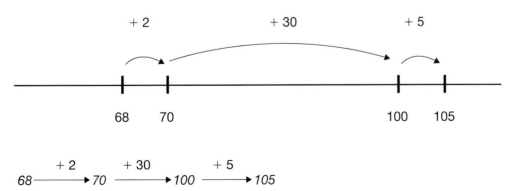

$$105 - 68 = 2 + 30 + 5 = 37$$

Figure 5.12 *105 – 68 using the number line*

This technique can be used for any subtraction calculation, and thus genuinely builds progression.

Multiplication and division

Although division can be seen as repeated subtraction, and the standard written method of long division reinforces this link, many children also use the links between multiplication and division to help them solve problems. Using the number line again, these links can be clearly illustrated:

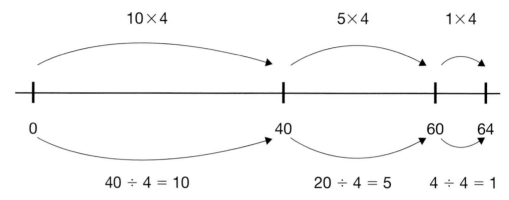

Figure 5.13 *Showing the links between multiplication (16 × 4 = 64) and division (64 ÷ 4 = 16)*

All division and multiplication calculations – through to large numbers and decimal fractions – can be represented in this way as a way of scaffolding children's understanding.

Other skills and understanding come into play:

- using known multiplication bonds, e.g. 10 × 4 = 40, 5 × 4 = 20, to bridge towards the product or dividend;

- the importance of estimating, e.g. in dividing 924 by 22, we could use 10 × 22 = 220 as a first step, but it would be worth progressing children onto estimating that 4 lots of 10 × 22 would be nearer 900, and a next step could be that 40 × 22 = 880.

Here, the number line is used as the basis for progression, from addition through its links with subtraction (or finding difference) and then using this understanding in multiplication and division. When progressing through to using negative integers, the same technique can still apply. Note, too, that the movement along the line is consistently from the smaller (sometimes zero) to the larger number, though of course when dealing with, say, −8 × 3, it might be better to visualise three steps moving in the negative direction.

The approach to calculation

To summarise, calculation is best addressed through enabling children to tackle problems mentally first, then, for more complex calculations, they can move on to informal presentations, such as the number line (or grid method for multiplication, illustrated below). Only when they fully understand what the calculation is about, and that they can use whatever method that works for them, is it useful for them to attempt to learn the standard methods. For example, given the multiplication 23 × 15, the three processes discussed above can be illustrated as follows:

Mental method

$$23 \times 15 = 23 \times 10 + 23 \times 5$$

23 × 10 = 230. 23 × 5 is half of this, so 23 × 5 = 115. 230 + 115 = 345

Many children, including those who have difficulties with mathematics, know how to multiply by 10. From this, the pattern that multiplying by 5 is half the result of multiplying by 10 can be established. These techniques can be practised as starters to the lessons. Clearly, other techniques will have to be adopted for multiplying by other numbers, such as multiplying by 4 and realising that that is equivalent to doubling and doubling again, but the key is that the confidence to handle numbers mentally is a crucial starting point in calculating.

Informal method

The common informal method for long multiplication is known as the grid or box method, where the numbers are partitioned (so that 23 becomes 20 and 3, and 15 becomes 10 and 5). The numbers are organised as in Figure 5.14:

×	20	3	
10	200	30	=230
5	100	15	=115
			345

Figure 5.14 *The grid or box method for long multiplication*

This method expands the calculation, making visible all its different parts. With a 2-digit by 2-digit multiplication, there are 4 mini-multiplications (20 × 10; 3 × 10; 20 × 5 and 3 × 5), each of which should be added together to make the total. Many children miss out some of the calculations, often multiplying the two units together, then the two amounts of tens, then adding.

Formal method (standard written algorithm)

In the standard presentation, these calculations are condensed, but it is worth making the comparison explicit to children who may just be able to use the method, so that they can see where the calculations come from. This comparison is shown in Figure 5.15:

×	**20**	**3**	
10	200	30	=230
5	100	15	=115
			345

23
× 15
115
230
345

Figure 5.15 *Comparing methods for multiplication*

Translating ideas into different learning media

Mel Lever (2003) describes a visual representation of the months of the year as a clock face, or as a twelve-pointed star:

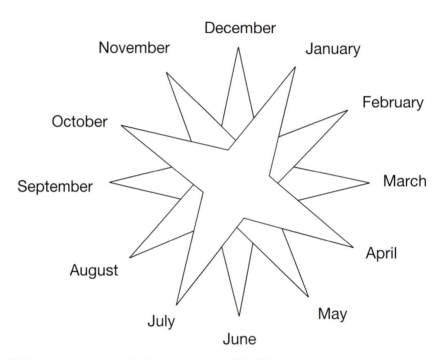

Figure 5.16 *The cycle of months in the year in a visual (clock) form*

Children could either use this visual representation to help understand the cycle of the year, and address questions about particular months, or relationships between the months (e.g. 'Which months are six months apart?') or they could place themselves physically in this arrangement. Other possibilities – dressing up appropriately for winter, spring, summer and autumn, and seating themselves in the right place then come into play; relationships between seasons (spring and autumn being opposite) can be explored, and the cycle of the year (e.g. counting four months from November goes into the next year, or counting on a number of years) can be discussed. Bruner (1996) describes narrative 'as a mode of thought and a vehicle for meaning-making'. Here are the tools for creating a story about time – a visual or physical image that can then be discussed, where children can make sense of the passage of the months from moving through them. Instead of a de-contextualised activity from a book, children have a tangible experience to refer to.

It would be easy to assume that most information transmitted between children and their teachers is in auditory form, and that we cater adequately for this preferred learning style in the normal course of events. However, there are activities that explicitly develop auditory skills, some of which highlight the desirability of working *between* preferred styles. This visualisation script is an example.

A visualisation script

The visualisation script given below is an example of a text that can be read to a class, with the intention of developing children's capacity to translate information given in one form (auditory) to another form (visual). Children are only asked to imagine an image, and alter it as per the instructions. Such modelling is an essential mathematical skill in interpreting problems in order to solve them.

Expected responses from children are given in bold:

Objective
Classify triangles (isosceles, equilateral, scalene) using criteria such as equal sides, equal angles, lines of symmetry (Year 5 objective).

Script
Imagine a square. Draw the diagonals from the opposite corners. Ask:

- What shapes do you have inside the square? **Triangles**

- What do you know about these triangles? **Isosceles, congruent, identical, two sides the same, two angles the same, two angles are 45°, the other is 90°.**

- How do you know this?

Other examples of 'visualisations' could be taken from the Framework supplement of examples (page 184) (DfES 2001). Children could alternatively draw their images on individual whiteboards – translating the auditory information to their own diagrams, which can be easily displayed. This allows the teacher to assess the child's understanding quickly.

Changing resources to change the mathematics in an activity

Prestage and Perks (2001) describe how planning an activity with different resources changes the nature of the mathematics that can be learned from it. As a simple example, consider how children might find the mid-point along the base of a wall in the classroom.

If the resources they were offered (or that they chose) were a tape measure and (possibly) a calculator, then the mathematics to be learned might be:

- Measure (and draw) lines to the nearest millimetre (Year 5 objective).

- Use doubling and halving (Year 5 – if children find the length of the whole wall and halve it).

- Check with inverse operations when using a calculator (Year 5 – checking their answer by doubling it again to get the total length).

- Identify the necessary information to solve a problem (Year 7 objective).

However, the mathematics will completely change if the resources offered to the children were only a stick (of no standard measurement, and without any calibrations) and perhaps a piece of string and a pencil, with which to find the mid-point of the base of the wall. Now the task is in the area of geometrical reasoning, because the solution lies in applying an understanding of symmetry. If pupils mark off several stick lengths, starting at each end of the wall, where they come to near the centre, they can then use the string between the two central marks, fold it in half and then lay it down to find the mid-point. The mathematics in this activity could be described through these objectives:

- Identify the necessary information to solve a problem (Year 7) and represent problems and interpret solutions in geometric form (Year 8).

- Find simple loci, by reasoning (Year 8).

In summary, considering different resources for preferred learning styles also opens up the opportunity for new and deeper understandings of mathematics to be explored.

Using colour

Colours can be used to emphasise or clarify patterns or links. For example, in helping children to develop their geometric reasoning skills, colours can highlight equal angles in sets of parallel lines (Figure 5.17).

Some questions that could accompany this activity could be:

- Colour in all the angles that have the same value. Use a different colour for different sized angles.

- How many different colours do you need?

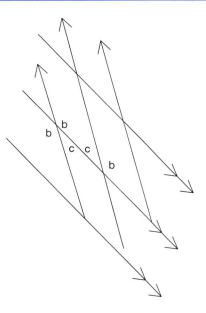

Figure 5.17 *Two sets of parallel lines, to help children highlight the fact that vertically opposite, corresponding and alternate angles are equal*

- Why only two?

- Does this have anything to do with the numbers of sets of parallel lines?

If a *third* set of parallel lines is added, which cut through the same points of intersection – how many colours are now needed?

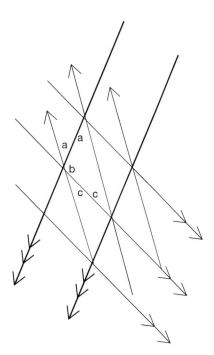

Figure 5.18 *Three sets of parallel lines, to illustrate that the three angles in a triangle match three angles on a straight line*

By colouring differently the angles marked a, b and c, the connections between the angles on the straight line and the angles in a triangle are highlighted. This is an important mathematical idea, generated from the use of colour, to clarify relationships within parallel lines, leading to a proof that the angles in a triangle sum to 180°. Such techniques make this level of mathematical understanding far more accessible than formal written methods.

Physical movement can be used to understand mathematical ideas

The topic of angles and bearings can be addressed in this way. For instance, we can ask the class to face north (assuming that we know which direction that is from your classroom!). Children could then be asked to face the other points of the compass together; or to turn a specific number of degrees; or to face particular bearings. This can reinforce the idea that bearings represent a clockwise turn from north, and help children estimate a range of angles. This gives a physical experience that an angle is a measurement of turn.

An understanding of co-ordinates can also be addressed in a similar way. Organising the group into a block, and assigning each child with co-ordinates, useful questions can be asked to allow children to experience patterns and rules in co-ordinates, e.g.:

- Stand up (or hands up) if your first number (x co-ordinate) is 2.

- Stand up (or hands up) if your second number (y co-ordinate) is 3.

- Stand up (or hands up) if your numbers are the same.

- Stand up (or hands up) if your two numbers add up to 7.

Each of these will produce straight-line answers – children can recognise these connections from their experience.

Structuring thinking

Spider diagrams – moving from the known to the unknown

Another example of using a visual presentation to structure thinking is in the use of 'spider' diagrams or concept maps. For example, using such a diagram (Figure 5.19) can build an understanding of finding decimal fractions of numbers. Starting from the centre, children could offer connected calculations and explain their links from the centre. Alternatively, the teacher could write in the link and ask children to calculate what should be the result.

These diagrams could also be used in many areas of mathematics, e.g. to help children manipulate algebraic expressions (Appendix 5.3), or to make links between fractions or percentages.

Using tables to solve problems

Organising information is an important mathematical skill, but it is also an essential teaching technique to help children who have difficulties with their mathematics.

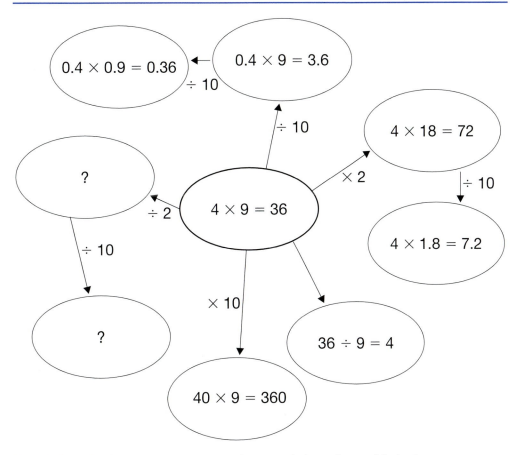

Figure 5.19 Spider diagram, using connections between whole numbers and decimals

There are many problems that create links involving multiplication – conversion problems (metric to metric, metric to imperial, and currency problems), percentages, scale drawings, fractions, ratio and proportion problems, and enlargements are just a few examples. Often such problems are presented in words, and most examples of solutions offered in texts are also written. However, many children can be helped if they are shown how to organise the information given into tables, so that the links between the numbers are clarified, e.g.:

'With every £10 I can buy 15 euros for my trip to France. I manage to save £60 to use as spending money. How many euros can I buy?'

Figure 5.20 shows how this information can be organised. Children should be asked about how to construct the table – what headings are needed, where to put the numbers 15 and 60, as well as what links the numbers. It is in the process of organising the problem that we find how to solve it.

Pounds	Euros
10	15
60	

× 6   × 6

Figure 5.20 Using a table to help solve a currency conversion problem

The calculation is now clarified – children are helped to see why they have to multiply the number of euros by 6.

The problem can be extended, e.g.:

'If I come back with 30 euros, how many pounds can I buy with this?'

The table is shown in Figure 5.21.

Pounds	Euros
10	15
60	90
	30

× 2   × 2

Figure 5.21 *Extending the problem*

Another example of this approach is illustrated in Appendix 4.5, where the metric conversions (e.g. answering such questions as how many centimetres are in a metre, etc.) are displayed alongside the familiar 'HTU' – hundreds, tens and units presentation of place value. Children should be invited to see patterns and predict entries into the table. This clarifies the connections within the number system, and helps children see the consistency in the design of the metric measurement systems we use.

Structuring writing

It can be argued that the emphasis in the three-part lesson on developing children's oral skills – explaining, justifying, reasoning, proving – goes a long way to addressing the development of children's 'mathematical' literacy. The importance placed on the development of children's reasoning skills is exemplified in the objectives such as:

- P7: Use mathematical language such as more or less, greater or smaller to compare given numbers of objects (DfES 2002); through

- Year 5: Explain methods and reasoning, orally and in writing; to

- Year 9: Present a concise reasoned argument, using symbols, diagrams, graphs and related explanatory text (DfES 2001).

Developing mathematical literacy

There is a distinction between the development of mathematical literacy and developing literacy skills through mathematics. Consider children explaining why the probability of getting a 'head' when tossing a coin is $\frac{1}{2}$. The language needed to explain this might include 'fair', 'even', 'equally likely', 'outcome', and so on – vocabulary which can be strategically placed on display so that children may refer to it in their explanations. We might, after some discussion, ask children to try to convince someone (a pen friend, a parent, etc.) *in writing* that the probability is $\frac{1}{2}$. Here is an opportunity to engage in the drafting process, to develop children's precision in using the vocabulary and capacity to construct a convincing argument – both of which are authentic tasks for mathematicians at any level.

The written pieces can be developed in a number of ways:

- The teacher could collect the pieces, and either copy some examples onto an OHT for the next class discussion, or piece together some parts of the writing, with the specific objective of developing clarity in the arguments. The class could together improve the writing and use of vocabulary.

- Children could pass their written pieces to each other, to see how well they understand each other's arguments. They could then review each other's work together and improve the writing.

Whichever method is used, it is founded on the drafting process to improve writing. Of course, ICT could be used effectively here, where children could form their first drafts using a wordprocessor, possibly print a hard copy and review it by themselves, with partners or with the whole class, and then return to improve the quality of their writing. The messages sent out by doing this are:

- We cannot expect to master everything – including writing – at the first go (Mason 1988).

- The first written draft does not have to be perfect – indeed, it is unlikely to be so.

- The quality of our work improves through the process of review and redraft.

There is a danger, in attempting to develop literacy skills through mathematics, in considering low-level skills and applying them falsely to a mathematical context, for example an exercise for pupils could look like this:

Complete these sentences:

- The . . . . of tossing a coin and getting a head is $\frac{1}{2}$.

- A head and a tail are equally likely . . . . from tossing a coin once.

These are simply written forms of the low-level 'guess what's in my head' questions, going little further than recalling knowledge of the particular words 'probability' (first sentence) and 'outcomes' (second sentence). Like many word-searches, such activities do not develop an understanding of the vocabulary, and how it should be applied to describe or to explain or to convince someone of an argument, which is arguably the purpose of being literate. These are not authentic tasks for mathematicians, and arguably do not help children *become* mathematicians.

If children genuinely have word-finding difficulties, it would be more effective for them to have ready and easy access to the vocabulary (either through display or through reference books or sheets) and a meaningful situation where they are required to use this vocabulary, such as in explaining their methods, describing shapes or patterns, justifying the rules they have discovered or reasoning about a mathematical situation.

On the other hand, writing and speaking frames (as exemplified in Chapter 4 and Appendices 4.15 and 5.4) help children with difficulties with mathematics to organise their thinking. These frames act as prompts to thinking about how children are going to solve problems, rather than testing recall of knowledge.

Teaching styles

The description of a collaborative structure to an episode of a lesson (for instance, the main activity) does not have to be incompatible with the focus on direct teaching promoted by the Framework (DfES 2001). The emphasis on an episodic structure allows for teachers to employ a range of teaching styles to suit the objectives of the lesson and the children's preferred learning styles.

There are a number of ways in which teaching styles have been described, so some clarification of the terms is necessary. Both 'traditional' and 'progressive' descriptions have been used pejoratively: 'traditional' for describing desks in ranks, silent classrooms, activities which focus on methodology rather than developing understanding, and teachers equating learning with transmission of knowledge; 'progressive' labelling may conjure up pictures of pupils wandering aimlessly about, little focused interaction with the teacher, and a lack of order and structure to the lessons. Perhaps neither term is an adequate description of what goes on in mathematics classrooms.

Certainly, neither style, as described above, helps children to learn effectively, especially those with SEN. These chapters have promoted the ideas that children learn through talk and action, characterised by purposeful collaboration and authentic, meaningful mathematical activities. If, in 'traditional' settings, children follow mechanistic routines and have limited opportunities to communicate their ideas – to exchange meaning – then the opportunities for understanding are similarly limited. Certainly, transmitting knowledge in a direct style is efficient and enables us to cover a curriculum, but there must be serious questions about whether children understand all that goes on. On the other hand, if in 'progressive' classrooms, activities are not followed by purposeful reflection, and the teacher takes little responsibility for developing progression in understanding, then again, the children's learning is restricted.

Quite simply, the best tack to take is to realise that different approaches or styles may be the most appropriate at certain times for certain pupils in certain situations. We should be looking to develop a repertoire of skills and approaches in the classroom – sometimes 'telling them' is both efficient and effective; other times children will need to handle mathematical equipment such as connecting cubes to understand a situation. Further opportunities to make links to other aspects of mathematics are essential – fractions and decimals form an integral part of understanding probability; exploring areas of rectangles can support an understanding of the commutative law of multiplication. Mathematics teachers will recognise when and how to make these links for individual pupils.

At the heart of considering teaching styles must lie an understanding of our values – not only what we believe about how children learn as described above in terms of talk and action, but also what it is they should learn. This latter point can be exemplified by the distinction of considering whether we are teaching children about mathematics (reflecting that the goal of learning is the acquisition of knowledge) or teaching children to become mathematicians (reflecting the participatory or situated model – 'learning and a sense of identity are inseparable' (Lave and Wenger 1991)). The former may lead us into believing that children learn through the transmission of knowledge; the latter may help us to recognise the importance of enabling children to handle mathematical vocabulary effectively in their own attempts at reasoning. Again, perhaps there is a place for both styles. However, if the inclusive classroom is one where children become empowered, then such empowerment can only come from developing their self-esteem, and this self-esteem arises from feeling that they understand, and that they belong in their community. On this view, coverage of a curriculum cannot be allowed to override an understanding of it.

Monitoring and Assessment

The purposes of assessment

In designing any assessment system, it is important to be clear about its purposes. A conflict of audience interests can impair the value of the assessment itself. The following provide a guide:

- to improve learning (by identifying both successes and misconceptions, and adjusting future teaching accordingly);

- to inform pupils of their progress;

- to inform parents of pupils' progress;

- school and teacher accountability.

Assessment systems intended to inform parents of student progress should look quite different from the methods of informing children. Children will need guidance on specific objectives, often on a day-to-day basis, and such advice may form part of plenary sessions of mathematics lessons, or comments when marking books. Such detail may not be necessary for parents, who may want a larger picture of progress, and therefore advice on more general ways they can help their children. Parents may be more interested in levels or grades but, as Black and Wiliam (1998) suggest in their discussion of formative assessment, these may be counterproductive when discussing progress with children. This will be dealt with more fully later in the chapter.

P levels, progression through to NC levels, using the National Numeracy Framework documents

There are three key documents in supporting progression and assessment, available for teachers in England:

- *Accessing the National Curriculum for Mathematics* (DfES) (0292/2002);

- *Framework for teaching mathematics – Reception to Year 6* (DfES 1999); and

- *Framework for teaching mathematics – Years 7, 8 and 9* (DfES 2001).

All three texts present supplements of examples of what children should be able to do and can therefore be used in conjunction to identify progression (see Chapter 4), and can support the development of an assessment system. For example, in 'Using and applying mathematics', the document suggests a possible outcome at level P7:

Respond to 'How many footballers are in the picture?' 'How many have blue shorts on?'

In looking at the Key Objectives from the Primary Framework in Year 1 (DfES 1999), we find:

Use mental strategies to solve simple problems using counting, addition, subtraction, doubling and halving, explaining methods and reasoning orally.

An activity to help meet this objective could be:

How many dots are there in total?
Explain how you work out your answers.

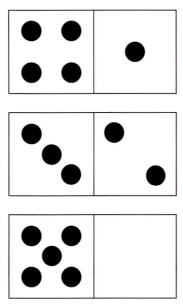

Some children may decide to count all 15 dots.
A more advanced technique would be to recognise that each domino has five dots, represented in three different ways: 4 + 1, 3 + 2, 5 + 0. Then, we could develop children's use of multiples of five, or counting in fives to find the total.

Figure 6.1 *An activity using counting strategies to find a total*

Whereas in the first example, children may simply be asked to count the number of footballers, Figure 6.1 shows an example where counting and adding strategies could be used to find the total. An essential feature of the activity is that children are asked to explain how they made their calculations. Although this may be an individual assessment task, conducted one-to-one with an adult, it may also be used as a learning task if conducted with more than one pupil, so that methods for solving the problem are compared.

Identifying progression in this way can be valuable in developing teachers' own understanding of the NC level descriptions as well as a clearer picture of children's progress.

How we assess

The Framework for teaching mathematics: Years 7, 8 and 9 (DfES 2001) states that:

Where *assessment* is concerned, better standards of mathematics occur when:

- pupils understand and are engaged in the assessment process;

- teachers use pupils' contributions to assess their strengths and difficulties, to set group and individual targets for pupils to achieve and to plan the next stage of work;

- assessments include informal observations, oral questioning and occasional tests or special activities designed to judge progress;

- recording systems give teachers the information that they need to plan and report successfully, but are not too time-consuming to maintain.

Our assessment of children's work is conducted through both written and oral forms, both informally and through formal testing.

Informal observations/Oral questioning

The quality of these assessments is directly related to the quality and nature of questioning. Here is the classification by Berger *et al.* (2000) again:

- recalling facts

- applying facts

- hypothesising and predicting

- designing and comparing procedures

- interpreting

- applying reasoning

Clearly, questions limited to the 'What are 6 × 8?' type only assess recall. A greater range of questions (such as those illustrated in Appendix 5.2) will offer teachers a better insight into children's understanding, and then enable teachers to think of learning activities that develop children's understanding further. The example given below of a lesson about finding percentages illustrates how such questioning can emerge from considering a problem-solving approach to teaching.

Although the plenary session of structured mathematics lessons is specifically designed to enable such informal assessments to take place regularly, it must be remembered that such questioning should take place throughout the various lesson episodes. Effective starters will reveal issues; teachers' or TAs' questions of individual pupils in the main activities will reveal misconceptions that can be addressed in whole-class discussions.

Marking, using formative assessment effectively in the classroom, and the impact of the choice of activity on assessment

Black and Wiliam (1998) argue that improving learning through assessment depends on:

- the provision of effective feedback to pupils;

- the active involvement of pupils in their own learning;

- adjusting teaching to take account of the results of assessment;

- a recognition of the profound influence assessment has on the motivation and self-esteem of pupils, both of which are crucial influences on learning;

- the need for pupils to be able to assess themselves and understand how to improve.

These considerations are true for all pupils.

It is also important to keep in mind that in just the same way that the quality of learning is directly affected by the choice of activity (Chapter 5, 'Know and use the order of operations' lesson), so the quality of our feedback to pupils is also affected by the nature of the activity we are assessing. The following example illustrates this point:

Method 1
To find a percentage of a quantity, you can change the percentage into a fraction or a decimal and multiply this by the quantity, e.g.:

Find 48% of 250
48% = 0.48. So 0.48 x 250 = 120

Calculate the following:
(i) 45% of 220   (ii) 22% of 50 kg   (iii) 75% of £480

Figure 6.2 Teaching percentages of a quantity from a given method

Children are often given pages of this sort of exercise, perhaps because of the belief that practising a given method ensures learning. However, this kind of presentation of the problem does not ensure understanding of what finding a percentage of a quantity means, and more importantly it does not help children understand how to apply the knowledge they already have. For example, they may already be confident in their own mental strategies for these calculations, by using the method shown later in this section (Figure 6.3).

What are the likely ways in which this exercise in Figure 6.2 would be marked or assessed? Some possibilities are described below:

- A page of ticks or crosses, presented as a fraction of correct answers, e.g. 7 out of 10. Note Black and Wiliam's (1998) concern that 'greater attention given to marking and grading, much of it tending to lower the self-esteem of pupils, rather than to providing advice for improvement and a strong emphasis on comparing pupils with each other which demoralises the less successful learners' are *inhibiting* factors to effective learning.

- Constructive comments – perhaps linked to how the pupils have attempted to use the method. This may be better, but can only be considered formative if children have an opportunity to apply their response to the comments as soon as possible. If such marking has taken place at the end of the work, the comments may not even be read, let alone used to improve learning, and the effort could be wasted.

- Comments related to children's presentation. Black and Wiliam (1998) also cite 'a tendency for teachers to assess quantity of work and presentation rather than the quality of learning' as another inhibiting factor for effective learning.

However, if we contrast this presentation of the task with an activity that is designed to build children's problem-solving strategies as well as their skills in handling percentages, we can immediately consider that the 'quality of learning' to which Black and Wiliam refer is enhanced.

Beginning with the centre of a spider diagram, a process can be modelled for pupils for finding percentages of the given number. This spider is illustrated in Figure 6.3.

However, the key question 'What is a good percentage to work with?' takes the lesson to another aspect of mathematics – examining strategies for solving problems. Given the objectives:

- find simple percentages of small whole-number quantities (Y6), or

- calculate simple percentages (Y7)

there is a danger of presenting children with an activity that only addresses these objectives in narrow ways, such as that given in Figure 6.2. However, this presentation goes further – involving objectives taken from 'Using and applying mathematics to solve problems' such as:

- Break a complex calculation into simpler steps, choosing and using appropriate and efficient operations and methods; and

- Identify the necessary information to solve a problem (Y7).

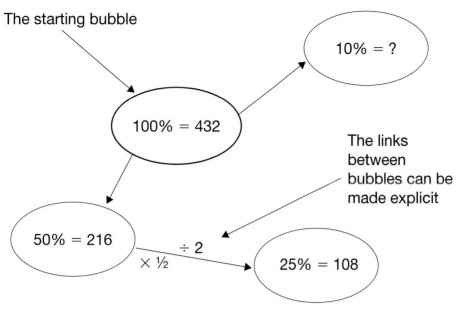

The starting bubble

10% = ?

100% = 432

The links between bubbles can be made explicit

50% = 216

÷ 2

× ½

25% = 108

Pupils can be organised into pairs, and invited to make up their own spider diagram of percentages from a new starting quantity. They can be challenged to find as many percentages of this quantity as they can.

In the plenary session pupils can be asked to apply their findings for a range of quantities and percentages, e.g.:

Present a table such as this:

Percentage	Quantity
25%	£6
15%	50g
1%	260
54%	45 miles

Combining any percentage with any quantity (there are therefore 16 different questions here), children can be asked to find the solution, and explain how they worked it out. The assessment that takes place here is immediate, and focused *not just on the answer, but the method of calculating.*

Figure 6.3 *A spider diagram method for presenting percentages of quantities*

This lesson works on the premise that children will learn effectively through engaging in an activity where they are part of the decision-making (they choose which percentages to find), where they work collaboratively in deciding and calculating, and where their engagement leads them to understand strategies for finding *any* percentage of *any* quantity. The key question highlights the strategy children are likely to use, and enables them to be clear about their problem-solving techniques. This is much more of a learning activity than giving the answers to a page of an exercise.

Black and Wiliam (1998) assert that:

Feedback to any pupil should be about the particular qualities of his or her work, with advice on what he or she can do to improve, and should avoid comparisons with other pupils.

Therefore, in implementing formative assessment techniques in the classroom, it is essential to keep in mind what we can be formative *about*. In the example given above, the assessment of children's work can be focused on their 'mathematical performance' – how they go about solving the problems, rather than on written outcomes (answers) to a page of questions. So, in finding a percentage of a given quantity, the mathematical performance rests on a range of skills:

TABLE 6.1 IDENTIFYING THE SKILLS USED WITHIN A SPECIFIC PROBLEM

Generic problem-solving skills	Skills specific to this problem
Clarifying the problem	By, for example, translating the problem to a number line, or other diagrammatic or physical representation. By identifying the key meanings from the problem, e.g. that finding a percentage less than 100% gives an answer less than the original; greater than 100% gives an answer that is greater than the original quantity.
Breaking the problem down into smaller, manageable parts	Breaking the percentage down into a series of manageable calculations.
Identifying the techniques needed to solve the problem	Possible techniques include: • Applying an understanding that *'of'* relates to multiplying; • Choosing to use fractions, decimals or percentage equivalents – e.g. '$33\frac{1}{3}$% of £12' is better translated into '$\frac{1}{3}$ of £12' to make a more efficient calculation; • Understanding that the value can be expressed as multiples of 10% + a multiple of 1%, • Understanding that the percentage can be expressed as a combination of other, easily calculable percentages – e.g. 26% = 25% + 1%.
Technical fluency	Doing the calculations accurately and efficiently: • Applying any of a range of appropriate calculating skills – e.g. halving quantities to find 50%, halving again for 25%; • Applying the understanding that finding 10% of a quantity is equivalent to dividing it by 10; • Dividing quantities by 10 and 100, by recognising the change in place value; • Finding multiples of 10% or 1%, and combining these results.

TABLE 6.1 *(continued)*

Strategic fluency, e.g.:
- Using tables of results, to establish links
- Finding patterns in results to predict later outcomes
- Using estimation to help decide the strategy for working, and for checking
- Choosing tools to assist, e.g. using a calculator for efficiency
- Checking

Estimating percentages, e.g. 48% of 220 must be just less than half of 220, about 110.
A table of results could be:

100%	220
10%	22
50%	110
25%	55
1%	2.2
24% (25% − 1%)	52.8 (55 − 2.2)
48% (24% × 2)	105.6 (52.8 × 2)

Finding ways of checking, e.g. translating percentages to fractions/decimals, estimating answers, using a calculator, finding alternative routes to an answer.

Evaluating the process

Evaluating the collaboration:

- How did we work together?
- What roles did we take?
- Were decisions made jointly?

Evaluating problem-solving techniques:

Would working with fractions be easier sometimes, e.g. for $33\frac{1}{3}$% it would be easier to find $\frac{1}{3}$ of the total instead of going through 10%, 1% and $\frac{1}{3}$%.

When feeding back information to pupils, therefore, we can analyse how they attempt to solve the problem, and then identify the steps they need to take to improve. These processes are included in the model of assessment offered in the appendices for this chapter (6.1–6.6).

In this case, it may be that the child has difficulty right at the start in clarifying what to do to solve the problem. It may also be that involving the child in translating the problem to a visual form, such as a number line, will help, e.g. Figure 6.4:

Find 40% of 220

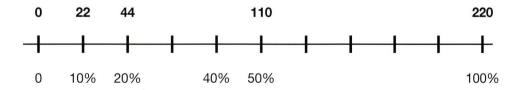

Figure 6.4 *Using a number line to represent a percentages problem*

The number line can be used for counting in twenty-twos, to reach 40%; it provides a visual illustration of what needs to be found.

Perhaps translating the problem into a table (as at the bottom of Table 6.1) would be an alternative, because it means that children are guided to find the salient information from the text.

The first question has to be *'What do you have to find out?'* followed by *'Can you present this information another way?'* If the child is still stuck, then there are clear teaching points illustrated, perhaps first by addressing how they might translate ideas into number lines or tables.

The marking of this type of work takes a different form from ticks and crosses and a mark out of ten. Here, we are led directly into making constructive comments, without the need for grades or marks. These comments will be related to structuring or scaffolding how the child goes about solving the problem, e.g. if they can tabulate results, can they then use the information to find links? Can they use the links to predict later numbers?

Pupil involvement

For children who have difficulties with their mathematics, formative assessment can be used as a powerful motivating force. Children who can clearly see *how* they are making progress enjoy their successes and are encouraged to sustain their efforts.

Part of the process is to engage children in assessing for themselves. This can be achieved through self-assessment or peer assessment. Conducted regularly, this process can help children understand more clearly what they have to do to succeed, and reflect on the ways in which they are working more effectively.

The lesson described above could take on an element of pupil self-assessment or peer assessment. The teacher, TA or pupil partners could ask which aspects of solving the problem they found hard, perhaps using the identification offered in Table 6.1 as a guideline. Children would become clearer themselves about how they are working and what progress they are making with regular experience of the generic statements:

- clarifying the problem

- breaking the problem down into manageable parts

- identifying the appropriate techniques to solve the problem

- technical fluency

- evaluating the process

The generic GCSE criteria can also be used in this way. The examination boards have published generic criteria to mark coursework tasks for GCSE assessment. When translated into pupil versions (see Appendix 6.6), these can be used in the classroom as the pupils are engaged in any 'Using and applying' (MA1) task. The assessment process could then take the following forms:

- As pupils are working on longer investigational or problem-solving tasks, the teacher (or TA) could discuss with pupils what they have achieved in their work, indicating this achievement on the criteria sheet. Targets could quickly be identified, either by using the criterion from the next level, or by looking at another strand.

- Pupils could attempt to assess their own work using the criteria. This mark could be compared with the teacher's assessment, and differences discussed. This process clarifies the criteria, and what constitutes evidence for achieving them.

- Pupils could mark each other's work. This process requires pupils to justify their assessments, which again develops their understanding of the criteria and their requirements. However, this process also needs to be monitored, and it may prove more useful once pupils have gained a certain amount of experience with the criteria.

Using these criteria has a more general application than GCSE coursework. The process can be adopted throughout Key Stage 3 as well as Key Stage 4; one of the purposes behind the coursework element of the GCSE is to enable pupils to solve longer mathematical problems successfully, and such use of the assessment criteria means that we are teaching children these processes effectively – whether they are taking an examination or not.

There is a further development of pupil self-assessment in the next section.

What do we assess?

The answer to this question is not confined to problem-solving strategies alone.

The Framework for Key Stage 3 (DfES 2001, pages 39–43) suggests developing a class record based on Key Objectives for medium-term assessments (assessments taken over a period of half a term). Although these may be useful for the majority of pupils working in the expected attainment range for the year group, such objectives may not appear so appropriate for children experiencing difficulties. For example, a Key Objective in Year 8 is:

Use standard column procedures for multiplication and division of integers and decimals, including by decimals such as 0.6 or 0.06; understand where to position the decimal point by considering equivalent calculations.

For some children with difficulties, developing mental or informal strategies for multiplication and division may be a more accurate and appropriate objective. The objectives for Year 8 are roughly placed at level 5. However, this is not to dismiss the Key Objectives for children with SEN, because they form a basis of entitlement. Our task is to find ways to address them meaningfully in our classrooms.

The problem for a teacher of children experiencing difficulties with mathematics is that the range of objectives appropriate for the class is likely to be very broad, taking in objectives from P levels through to the National Curriculum levels appropriate for that age range. This will have the likely effect of producing an assessment system that is too large to manage. Even with the support of the DfES documents (1999, 2001, 2002) we produce long lists of progressive objectives, as in Chapter 4's list of objectives for 'Handling Data'. It may be worth considering an assessment system focused on the *likely* areas of difficulty, so that we can identify children's progression with the most fundamental aspects of mathematics.

Berger *et al.* (2000) have identified the following key mathematical concepts for children with learning difficulties, especially at Key Stage 2:

- number, including cardinality and ordinality

- counting, including one-to-one correspondence

- operation of combining and partitioning

- comparing two numbers

- concepts of length, mass, capacity, time and money

- comparing two quantities

- classification of 2D and 3D shapes

- mathematical pattern

- concept of having properties or attributes

- classification by criteria

- position, direction and movement

These concepts form the basis of an understanding of number, but some also encourage an understanding in other aspects of mathematics. For example, an understanding of mathematical pattern will show itself in work on shape and space, such as tessellations and symmetry, but it is also an important feature of algebra – number sequences – and in handling data, the concept is further developed in looking at trends in graphs and tables.

At Key Stages 3 and 4 the specified curriculum is wider, with a greater emphasis on using and applying mathematics, algebra and handling data, and we should also consider the following concepts as major objectives in understanding mathematics:

- complements to 'useful' numbers, e.g. 10, 100, 1000 and multiples of these; also to 0.1 and 1 when calculating with decimals;

- place value, linked with the effect of multiplying by 10, 100, 1000 and decimal fractions;

- multiples – the times tables; and linked with this

- the relationships between the four arithmetic operations, and the links to algebra;

- using appropriate vocabulary to describe mathematical situations; and

- applying effective strategies to solve problems.

The latter two concepts do not imply discrete lessons. The effective use of vocabulary and application of problem-solving strategies should become a feature of all lessons, but, since assessment tends to drive the curriculum, it is important to highlight their place in an assessment system.

It is suggested that those children who have difficulties in their mathematics tend to have difficulties in some or all of the concepts described. What follows is a way of using this understanding in devising an assessment system to help identify progress in these Key Concepts. However, it is not intended to illustrate an assessment system for all children with special educational needs, but a model from which to work. An individual record sheet should be just that – one that is increasingly tailored to identify progress for that individual. The most effective teaching is responsive, and this process is better aided by clearer descriptions of children's progress.

Appendix 6.1 illustrates how we may translate these important concepts into National Curriculum level statements, and teaching objectives. The objectives are taken across the range of the National Curriculum levels, and across the attainment targets – 'Using and Applying', 'Number and Calculations', 'Algebra', 'Shape, Space and Measures' and 'Handling Data', and therefore they highlight both the entitlement and progression for all children at Key Stage 3.

Objectives may be added or removed – it is not suggested that this is a comprehensive list, but merely a guideline for consideration.

Individual pupil progress sheet

From this, it may be fairly straightforward to design a pupil individual record sheet, based on these Key Concepts. Appendix 6.2 keeps the statements in view, and they can be highlighted when the teacher is confident of a child's understanding. It also meets the requirement of 'recording systems that give teachers the information that they need to plan and report successfully, but are not too time-consuming to maintain'.

The progression may not be sufficiently detailed on these sheets to illustrate simply where the child is going next – again, referring to the teaching objectives (DfES 1999, 2001, 2002) will define these objectives more closely, and they can be added where necessary. As a record sheet, it will offer the teacher a reference for reporting and lesson planning, and if made available to the TAs, their comments could also contribute to these processes. An example of how the sheet could be used in this way is offered in Appendix 6.3, which offers an example of a partially completed sheet. This is not a tick-list – if we are assessing understanding, then we hope to see the child demonstrate that understanding in a variety of contexts. The comments could indicate in which contexts the children have been successful and in which not.

Pupil self-assessment

It follows that pupils can also be involved at this level of reflection on their learning. Appendix 6.4 offers an example of a pupil self-assessment sheet, which uses the increasingly common 'traffic light' system found in schools where children indicate if they are confident they understand (green), not quite sure (amber) or 'don't get it at all' (red). Other schools use a numbered system in a similar way (e.g. 1 = confident, 2 = not sure or 3 = do not understand), or qualitative categories such as 'beginning', 'achieving' and 'succeeding'. The statements to trigger the reflection are the main teaching objectives from lessons over a term/half-term, or Key Objectives (DfES 1999, 2001, 2002). In the example given, the statements are taken from the assessment system developed through this chapter. Children may use colours to indicate their assessment, or they may tick the relevant section of the sheet. When children have to deal with the objectives and the language within them in this way, it provides another opportunity for them to understand what the language means, and clarifies what they have to do to succeed.

Target setting, contributing to reviews and using Individual Education Plans (IEPs)

Working in this way with objectives, NC levels and structured assessment enables the teacher to contribute effectively to the IEP review process. By identifying progression carefully, the assessment statements become signposts to a child's development: teachers, pupils, TAs and the parents are clearer about the child's achievements and the next steps. Further, the statements go well beyond the more common targets of technical fluency, e.g. '*Know the 2×, 5× and 10× tables*', '*Add two 2-digit numbers involving carrying*'. Whereas such fluency is an essential ingredient of a mathematician's qualities, they by no means describe the whole, and such objectives stated at the exclusion of developing a child's capacity to use and apply mathematics may reinforce the notion of providing an exclusively skills-based diet for these children. In so doing, we are in danger of ignoring many of the child's difficulties with mathematics.

Specific objectives can be extracted from the assessment sheets that are considered to be fundamental to the child's mathematical development, and thus may form the focus of the IEP. Nevertheless, the whole of the assessment system describes the ongoing plan for the child: it considers the range of mathematics, and the expected progress in terms of clear objectives. IEPs typically identify the difficulties the child experiences with learning, and the strategies to help children achieve the stated objectives. These include resources, taking account of time and staffing needed to help. These might be additional to the allotted time for mathematics in the school's timetable, but it is important to allow for time within the timetable, and with the mathematics teacher for the child to achieve the targets. Setting targets for children is not a process for delegating full responsibility: if the child has to learn to 'Read and plot co-ordinates in the first quadrant' as part of the IEP, then it is only fair that there are clear plans for lessons on 'Position, direction and movement' to address this objective during the stated period.

Appendix 6.5 offers an example not of an IEP sheet, but of how the Key Concepts and assessment objectives translate readily into an identification of the specific difficulties and thus the IEP targets for the child. This example then shows some possible strategies and achievement criteria. It is often troublesome for teachers to identify a convincing demonstration of understanding within the achievement criteria. Often, a child doing a task successfully a number of times is seen as an acceptable demonstration of understanding. Gardner and Boix-Mansilla (1994) suggest that:

> one can conclude that genuine understanding has been achieved if an individual proves able to apply knowledge in new situations, without applying such knowledge erroneously or inappropriately; and he or she can do so spontaneously, without specific instruction to do so.

The achievement criteria given in Appendix 6.5 attempt to show examples of these 'new situations'.

Qualifications and examinations, GCSE, alternative accreditation

Any discussion about alternative accreditation must first address the question of expectations. The GCSE was established as a way of identifying achievement for the vast majority of pupils – many of whom would have statements for special educational needs. There are very few children for whom the GCSE Mathematics course is inappropriate. As a guide, the GCSE grade G is roughly equivalent to a National Curriculum level 4, whereas a Certificate of Achievement (Entry Level) course indicates attainment below that level. If children have already achieved a level 3 at Key Stage 3, then they are clearly entitled to undertake a GCSE course, so that they can continue to progress. There are also children who achieve below the level of the tests at KS3, but still pass a GCSE in KS4. It's hard work, but these successes are significant features of many schools throughout the country.

The QCA has produced assessment tasks for pupils working below the level of the tests, i.e. at level 2 or below. These can be downloaded from the QCA website (www.qca.org.uk). They are useful tools to help teachers assess pupils' progress.

Entry-level qualifications

As the first level of the National Qualifications Framework (NQF), entry-level qualifications indicate attainment broadly in line with National Curriculum levels 1, 2 and 3. The qualifications available at this level include basic skills such as adult literacy and numeracy as well as National Curriculum subjects such as English, science and mathematics. These qualifications are therefore applicable to a wide range of people – from 14 to adult, including those with SEN. The courses are run in schools, often as a one- or two-year programme in Years 10 and 11, but the courses are also run in residential care settings, prisons, young offenders' institutions and FE colleges.

At least 40% of entry-level certificates are assessed externally, through tests or assignments. For pupils for whom these forms of assessment are not appropriate, there are no nationally recognised alternatives.

Special arrangements or considerations for examinations

This is the source of many dilemmas for teachers, as well as quite a lot of paperwork. There are pupils who will clearly struggle in an examination setting, and for many it may be that they have such difficulty with reading the questions, that their chances of doing the mathematics is inhibited.

Pupils are entitled to special arrangements if it can be shown that the process of assessment through examinations inhibits their capacity to demonstrate their ability within the subject. For example, those pupils who have a specific learning difficulty, which perhaps shows itself in being unable to read questions from a paper independently, yet have throughout their school careers demonstrated high levels of mathematical understanding, are entitled to special arrangements. These must be appropriate for the child, and within that child's experience. The child might therefore just need extra time, may need a larger print version of the paper, or may need a reader or a scribe. Whatever support they have for the examination, it is essential that the child has had previous experience of it in a similar situation (i.e. internal examinations).

Clearly the corollary to this is that if the examination setting does not unduly inhibit the child's capacity to demonstrate understanding, then special arrangements are not applicable. If the child's reading, problem-solving and mathematical skills are all weak, then the examination will demonstrate this, and it will do so fairly.

Preparing pupils for tests and examinations

There is much we can do to help pupils with SEN prepare for any examinations or tests. Revising for mathematics is most effective through developing experience at problem-solving. It involves a range of skills – extracting information, translating this into another meaningful form, selecting an appropriate operation or other mathematical technique and checking results. As Mason (1988) points out: 'It is virtually impossible to read mathematics – it has to be done, to be worked through with pencil and paper.' This is certainly true of revision, and so the best revision technique is to regularly look at test questions and discuss them with pupils, so that they can unravel their meanings, and make their own decisions about solving them. Certain techniques have proved successful for many teachers in the past, including:

- Regular extra sessions, staffed both by teachers and teaching assistants, focused on solving test questions. These sessions could be during registration times, after school or lunchtimes. Some schools hold Saturday sessions for pupils, and these have the effect of raising the status of the examinations. For some children, getting them to believe that the qualifications have a genuine value is an important step.

- Special event days – again either on Saturdays, during holiday periods or as a planned whole day within school time, staffed by mathematics teachers and assistants, focused on how we solve the problems.

The main feature of both these types of event is that children *discuss how to solve the problem.* There is little value in setting up these situations if the child then has to engage with a test paper individually and silently and without support. Through discussion, children begin to know what they know, and will be more likely to demonstrate that understanding independently in the real examination.

CHAPTER 7

Managing Support

Teaching assistants in classrooms

Berger *et al.* (2000) suggest that the main role of the TA is to facilitate the inclusion of all pupils within the class.

A survey of the management of TAs in schools defined what makes good practice in the work of TAs by saying that effective practice:

- fosters the participation of pupils in the social and academic processes of a school

- seeks to enable pupils to become more independent learners

- helps to raise standards of achievement of all pupils

    (Centre for Educational Needs, University of Manchester, *The Management, Role and Training of Learning Support Assistants,* DfEE 1999)

Clearly these factors support inclusive practice: pupil participation, independence and their resulting higher achievements enable them to become empowered. Taking each of these points in turn, the practice of managing support in mathematics classrooms can be analysed.

Pupil participation

Participation can be seen in two ways – engaging with the activities of the lesson, and interacting socially with others during these activities.

TAs can play an important role in facilitating access to activities, through support with:

- **Organisation** – being prepared for the lesson/homework; structuring problem-solving;

- **The use of mathematical equipment** – e.g. calculators, protractors, compasses, etc.;

- **Reading and interpreting written material** – TAs could help children translate written problems into their preferred learning styles – part of the process of solving problems is to understand them, and children may understand written problems better if they are helped to create diagrams or physical interpretations of the problems;

- **Taking notes from the board**;

- **Supporting pupils in contributing to class discussions** – often, pupils like to validate their responses to an adult before speaking out to the whole class;

- **Keeping pace with the lesson** – TAs could help children with setting out their work if this aspect holds up the pace of their learning. If, for instance, drawing out the framework of a table of results is not the objective for learning, but its completion prevents the child engaging with the real work, a TA could speed up the process by helping to set the table out.

Fox and Halliwell (2000) also suggest that the TA can help by:

- Helping the pupils understand the sequence needed to complete the task (being careful that the learning is not defined by completion!). The goal is participation, and often this will conflict with a goal of 'having a completed product';

- Helping the pupil in knowing where to find relevant information (and how to use it);

- Helping the pupil to catch up with missed work.

If the goals for participation are concerned with acting socially, efforts in planning need to be made to identify effective groups, and also the purposes for their collaboration. TAs should have a role in this planning, and then in helping children with this socialisation, such as modelling taking turns to speak and listening to others. Depending on the size of the class, the TA could be involved in supervising the work of one (or more) group(s) while the teacher manages other groups. Mathematics activities such as problem-solving or extended investigations would fit well into this model, because the purposes of the collaboration centre on joint problem-solving. Such working also implies that the traditional model of classroom layout – separate desks – may not be appropriate.

It is essential to remember that the teacher should be modelling the questioning and the behaviour management strategies for the classroom for the TA. This would be more effectively addressed if both adults were in the same room. Therefore essential aspects of classroom management – keeping children on task, spotting early signs of disruption – are shared. This again implies that the role of the TA in that classroom has been clearly defined and agreed, so that both teacher and TA know how each should act in any given situation. This is an act of empowerment for the TA – responsibilities are shared, and there should be a mutual respect for the role of each adult.

The role of the TA in the structured mathematics lesson

Within the structured mathematics lesson – of starter, main activity and plenary – the TA could have a range of tasks. However, it is important – even if meetings with the TA are restricted by timetable or contractual constraints – that the objectives and outcomes for the lesson are made clear for all – TA and pupils. This would at least enable the TA to be clear about what needs to be achieved in a lesson, and what that achievement should look like. Without this guidance, TAs are left to pick up the ideas as best they can, and their interpretations of a task – just as with any person who may not be an expert mathematics teacher – may differ from the teacher's intentions, through no fault of their own.

The oral and mental starter

Often this may be considered a difficult part of the lesson to plan for active involvement of another adult, as many teachers manage the whole-class discussion alone, but there are many possibilities for TA involvement. The first issue to overcome is to examine the nature of the starter, i.e. does it necessarily imply rapid question and answers? Such sessions only involve recall, rather than developing thinking, but if a TA were present in the class, they could help children discuss their own methods for calculating, or reasons for interpreting data, and so on, as a precursor to the child responding to the whole class. This could extend the teacher's approach to managing discussions. All pupils could be given an opportunity to explain their reasoning to a partner first for half a minute or so, before addressing the whole class.

The main activity

Even if the main activity were not focused on problem-solving but, say, developing a new skill, requiring some practice, the TA can still enable children to participate effectively in the task, by being another 'expert' learner to support children through effective questioning of their understanding of the skills used. Again, the TA would need to be briefed on the strategies to support the mathematical thinking. For example, if the child were asked to calculate 30×40, the TA might need to ask the child how this links with the calculation 3×4, and focus on the principle of using mental strategies as a first resort, rather than take the child through a long multiplication.

Plenary

The TA as well as the teacher should understand the purposes of the plenary session. If children are being asked to reflect on their learning, the TA may have a role in aiding that reflection with a child or small group, even acting as scribe to support their contributions to a whole-class discussion. Alternatively, the plenary may be used as preparation for the next lesson, and it might support the children to discuss some vocabulary with the TA to help them prepare.

Assessment and evaluation

The TA's role in the class is different from that of the teacher and therefore offers a valuable alternative perspective on learning. Joint evaluations of the success of any activities in the lesson can be discussed, perhaps in relation to specific pupils. The TA may have a clearer insight into how pupils tackled a problem from working closely with them, and could therefore illustrate misconceptions or flaws in children's methods. This process makes planning for subsequent lessons more effective.

Independent learners

Independence has long been a goal of teachers of children with SEN. It may be further described as being able to solve problems, being able to cope or succeed in all aspects of learning independently. If seen with these perspectives, it becomes clear that the link to pupil participation is strong, but also independence is concerned with developing the pupil's capacity for decision-making.

Decision-making by pupils can be inhibited or enhanced by the type of activities through which children learn their mathematics (note the percentage activity in Chapter 6) and also by the types of discussion with which the child engages with teachers or assistants. It is essential that both teachers and TAs are clear about the kinds of questioning which will enable children to make their own decisions about their mathematics. Too often, we feel pressure to help children solve particular problems, or 'finish their work' – especially by false deadlines like the bell at the end of the lesson, and then we fall back on 'giving children methods that work'.

It is even more difficult to allow children with difficulties with their mathematics the space and time to articulate their own ideas about how they could solve problems, but if children are regularly given a complete structure by adults and only have to engage with the mechanics of calculations then they cannot achieve 'independence'. On this view greater independence is achieved through *increased* participation in the activities of mathematicians – mathematicians make their own (independent) decisions about which information to collect, which calculations to make, how to present their results, and so on. The notion that understanding can be deferred, i.e. that children mechanically process methods they are given, with the hope that at some later stage in their lives they will come to understand it, is simply a deferring of teachers' responsibility to help children understand.

All the examples offered in these chapters illustrate how we help children understand their mathematics, whether it is the *structure* of the mathematics (e.g. understanding the number system by the use of number lines), or the *purposes* of it (e.g. looking at misleading graphs and charts to identify why we present information in certain ways).

To develop children's independence, therefore, also requires teachers and TAs to be clear about the stages of problem-solving – it is through this analysis that we can best find specific targets for children's learning (see Chapter 6).

An example of how different kinds of conversations which surround children's problem-solving affect the development of their independence could be seen as follows:

Problem – to find a way of adding 14 + 16.

The child is stuck on this problem.

TABLE 7.1 VERSION A – QUESTIONS THAT KEEP THE CHILD DEPENDENT ON SUPPORT FOR LEARNING

Conversation	Commentary
Adult: You can write the sum down like this: 14 +16	Already, the adult takes the first decision. Is the child ready for standard column addition? Does the child understand what addition means? Does the child recognise patterns in, say, 4 + 6, 14 + 6, 14 + 16, and could therefore be encouraged to tackle this mentally?
What's the answer to six add four?	The child may or may not respond accurately, but if finding complements to ten is not the difficulty, then it may be that the child's difficulty lies in understanding the problem, or setting it out into a form that the child understands, or in other aspects of calculating, e.g. what to do with the extra ten. It may be better to focus questions on these aspects, rather than only getting children involved at this mechanical level.

TABLE 7.1 (CONTINUED)

Conversation	Commentary
Well done! 4+6 is ten, so we put the zero down here and carry the one. $$\begin{array}{r} 14 \\ +16 \\ \hline 0 \\ \scriptstyle 1 \end{array}$$	Here, the decision about setting out the sum has again been taken away from the child, so there can be no analysis of the child's understanding of where to place the zero or the ten. Many children reverse the digits, as if they are writing 10 in the wrong order: $$\begin{array}{r} 14 \\ +16 \\ \hline 1 \\ \scriptstyle 0 \end{array}$$ This can be dealt with more effectively when we ask the questions 'Where should we place the digits of 10?' and 'Why should we put them in these places?'
Good! What's three ones? So we can put the three there – $$\begin{array}{r} 14 \\ +16 \\ \hline 30 \\ \scriptstyle 1 \end{array}$$	It's not three ones – it's three tens. It's no wonder some children have difficulties with numbers if they are regularly described incorrectly.

Some questions need addressing:

- What role has the child played in this activity?

- To what extent has the child participated in solving the problem?

TABLE 7.2 VERSION B – QUESTIONS THAT DEVELOP INDEPENDENT THINKING

Conversation	Commentary
Adult: What does the problem say? What do you think you have to work out? Can you use a diagram or equipment to help you, e.g. a number line?	The stages of problem-solving can offer a guideline for questioning. Understanding the problem – extracting useful data, knowing what it is that has to be found, translating the problem into another medium, e.g. visual form using a number line. Planning the problem, e.g. knowing what calculations to use, finding how the problem can be broken down into manageable parts. Doing the calculations. Evaluating/checking.

TABLE 7.2 (CONTINUED)	
Conversation	**Commentary**
Where should you place the 14 on the number line? How could you show that you are adding 16 on this number line?	The adult of course must make decisions about how much scaffolding to offer – if the child has no clue about some of the tools to use, it may be necessary to remind them of number lines, Diene's blocks or counting sticks. However, the questions may still be asked so that children could make decisions about how to use them in their calculations.
How could you use these (Diene's) blocks to show 14? How could you add 16?	
What other ways could we do this calculation?	There are a range of methods, e.g. the mental ones, including partitioning $14 + 16 = 10 + 4 + 10 + 16$ and re-ordering $= 10 + 10 + 46 = 10 + 10 + 10 = 30$
How can we check if the result is correct? Which method is best for you?	By using alternative methods or by reversing the calculation: $30 - 16 = 14$

These questions clearly demand a wide-ranging understanding of the subject, as well as a good working relationship with the child. The expectations of the standard of a TA's work are very high on this model. Such a model may also imply:

- The teachers in the mathematics department model the questioning techniques – therefore a high percentage of the TA's time is spent in class with mathematics teachers, to expedite the TA's professional development.

- Lessons are carefully planned together; TA feedback on how a child has fared with the stages of problem-solving is an essential planning tool for future lessons.

Raising the standards of achievement for all pupils

Apart from the strategies discussed above, which are clearly designed for raising pupils' achievement, TAs could also have a role in:

- developing resources

- increasing pupil contact time

- managing the pupil experience in school

If TA contracts are managed effectively, their hours could be organised to increase pupil contact with adults. Opportunities can be created for extra sessions at lunchtimes, after school or during registration times for specific support, for example spending time with Year 11 children to discuss examination paper questions, or one-to-one support for children on specific mathematical targets – perhaps using the DfES Mathematics Challenge materials (DfES 2003) in Years 7 and 8.

TA time could also be used for developing resources for learning, e.g. posters on the different types of graphs or charts children could use to present results, along with the reasons for their choices, or other posters as per the appendices for Chapter 4. Other resources can be developed specifically for individual children. Time needs to be allocated for this purpose, and therefore TAs need not be timetabled full-time in classes.

Managing the support – a whole-school view

Strategic plans for managing support would look first at its aims, and then define the staffing and other resources needed to meet these aims. This view differs from an approach that may look at the hours 'donated' by LEAs, often linked to particular pupils, and then employing TAs to match those hours.

The main focus lies in the planning of the support, identifying the amount of staff hours that are required to provide it, and then the school taking the decision to employ those staff from its overall budget. It gives a clear indication by the school of its commitment to the support and how it should be deployed; it also gives a clear commitment to developing the qualities of its entire staff. In the past, too many staff may have lost hours associated with children at short notice, and their expertise in supporting a wider range of children is also lost. This is no way to employ people, let alone develop the quality of the support. Effective management of the support team would be concerned with developing TA expertise.

This expertise falls into two clear strands – subject knowledge and knowledge of the pupils – which are affected directly by the deployment of support staff. If the team were employed within departmental/subject areas, then clearly the responsibilities for development of the knowledge of the subject lie there. The difficulty would be that neither the teaching staff nor the TAs would have a holistic view of the child, and so there need to be regular opportunities for TAs and teachers to discuss and evaluate teaching strategies for particular children.

Conversely, if TAs are associated with particular year groups, there are clear benefits for using their understanding of the children. For example, they can advise teaching staff on appropriate teaching strategies for individuals, and on learning styles, they can contribute to review meetings with children and parents, and they can feed these views back to teachers. However, their experience will be *across* the curriculum, and the development of their own subject knowledge will be inhibited. The onus will then be on teachers to communicate teaching strategies effectively with TAs within each subject. Often, the problem is that there are no mutually convenient times for joint planning. TA contracts are not drawn up with collaborative planning in mind, and a picture of 100% TA contact time is common, although arguably less effective. A contact sheet might be useful, although this may not need to differ from the planning sheet (Appendix 4.2) which enables the TA and teacher to see the structure, objectives and key questions of the lesson, and offers an opportunity for the TA to feed back any useful comments about the children's experiences, to inform future planning. Clearly this requires mutual professional respect, which is worth cultivating.

This model of managing support rests on working in partnership. The learning environment we seek to create works for everyone within it – primarily for the pupils, but also for the teachers and the TAs. The inclusive, problem-solving classroom includes us all; the problem we are solving is 'How can we best help our children learn effectively?' This partnership with TAs is a valuable tool with which to solve that problem.

Real Pupils in Real Classrooms

Introduction

Although the previous chapters offer many examples of useful questions, activities and resources that can be used in the mathematics classroom, the real task is applying these ideas to children's learning. There follow some brief case studies, each focusing on a particular area of special educational need, through which the techniques discussed in the previous chapters are exemplified. Each one follows the same format with three sections: 'You will need to find out', 'You should consider' and 'Some strategies you/the TA could try'.

Teachers may find these examples useful to promote discussion in team meetings, either as a mathematics team, or in discussions between individual teachers, including the SENCO and TAs.

These case studies do not represent an exhaustive list – either of the range of special educational need or of the strategies that may work for children. They are intended to offer starting points for ideas for teachers and TAs to consider and try, and then develop after evaluating their impact on the children's progress.

Kuli, Year 8; Hearing impairment

Kuli has significant hearing loss. He has some hearing in his right ear but is heavily reliant on his hearing aid and visual cues ranging from lip reading to studying body language and facial expression to get the gist and tone of what people are saying. He often misses crucial details. Reading is a useful alternative input and his mechanical reading skills are good, but he does not always get the full message because of language delay. He has problems with new vocabulary and with asking and responding to questions.

Now in Year 8, he follows the same timetable as the rest of his class for most of the week but he has some individual tutorial sessions with a teacher of the deaf to help with his understanding of the curriculum and to focus on his speech and language development. This is essential but it does mean that he misses some classes, so he is not always up to speed with a subject.

He has a good sense of humour but appreciates visual jokes more than ones which are language based. He is very literal and is puzzled by all sorts of idioms. He was shocked when he heard that someone had been 'painting the town red' as he thought this was an act of vandalism! Even when he knows what he wants to say he does not always have the words or structures to communicate accurately what he knows.

Everyone is very pleasant and quite friendly to him but he is not really part of any group and quite often misunderstands what other kids are saying. He has a learning assistant which, again, marks him out as different. He gets quite frustrated because he always has ideas that are too complex for his expressive ability. He can be very sulky and has temper tantrums.

You will need to find out:

The extent of Kuli's hearing loss, and how he can take part in discussion

Kuli may have a radio-mike system that connects directly to his hearing aid, and so he may have some access to the class discussion. Usually, the teacher would wear the microphone around the neck. However, if pupils contribute good ideas to share, it may be appropriate that the teacher allows the child to speak through the microphone so that Kuli is fully included. Clearly, this may slow down the pace of the lesson, and such discussions will have to be managed carefully, but Kuli's needs may have a beneficial effect on the classroom culture, because there will be a genuine, clear need for turn-taking, and allowing others to speak clearly.

Alternatively, Kuli may take enough information from a combination of lip reading and his hearing aid. This will necessitate a change in the classroom layout when discussions take place – perhaps a circular layout so that everyone sees each other when speaking.

Find time to listen carefully to Kuli, to understand how he enunciates words. This will be essential when, in whole-group settings, you ask him to contribute ideas.

You should consider:

How to overcome the problem of Kuli's restricted access to handling mathematical vocabulary

The development of Kuli's use of mathematical vocabulary will be central to his overall progress in mathematics. It will not be picked up incidentally. The strategies below should help.

Planning with the TA

All of the following strategies should be discussed with the TA, including the TA's role with the whole class, rather than just with Kuli. It is worth being aware that having a TA constantly at his side may have the effect of *excluding* Kuli from the general run of the class, and a TA's support is in addition to the interactions Kuli will have with the teacher, not a substitute for them. To compensate for the extra attention Kuli may need in order to communicate with the teacher, the TA can be used to monitor the progress of other pupils in the class.

Some strategies you/the TA could try:

Developing vocabulary

- When planning key questions for lessons – or more likely, a series of lessons, especially those questions that are to be discussed as a whole class, they could be written (or typed) beforehand, so that Kuli can consider his responses carefully.

- Prepare vocabulary lists for lessons, to which the teacher, TA and the children can refer during any conversations. These will act both as a visual prompt for the whole class, as well as giving Kuli a clearer idea of what is being discussed.

- The same vocabulary lists should be shared with Kuli and the TA beforehand, so that they can prepare for lessons together, if such time is available. Again, this practice could involve the whole class – the plenary session for one lesson could be used as a vocabulary preparation for the following lesson.

Using alternative learning media

Written questions can be translated into algebraic, visual or physical forms. This is not just a question of access, but also develops greater insight into the mathematics. For example, the question '*What two numbers have a sum of 9 and a product of 20?*' could also be represented as:

$$a + b = 9, \qquad ab = 20, \qquad a = ? \qquad b = ?$$

Here the question is represented algebraically, and in so doing, this enables us to teach children how algebra is used to express unknowns, and how it can be derived from words.

Chapter 5 discusses different learning styles, and offers details of the use of number lines and other visual/physical techniques.

Plan with the TA how diagrams, algebra or physical resources might be used as alternative ways of expressing ideas, and prepare these in advance for Kuli to use in lessons. It is highly likely that this translation of ideas will benefit many more – if not all – children in the class.

Kuli's expressive language

If Kuli contributes to the class, but has difficulty in finding words, indicate that it is valid to express himself through diagrams or algebra. You could try to model his responses via diagrams – an example of this is given in Chapter 5, when illustrating how a child calculates 8×7, and the teacher 'translates' the calculation onto a number line. Kuli may be able to use the board himself for this purpose.

Harry, Year 7; Specific learning difficulties

Harry is a very anxious little boy and although he has now started at secondary school, he still seems to be a 'little boy'. His parents have been very concerned about his slow progress in reading and writing and arranged for a dyslexia assessment when he was aged 8. They also employ a private tutor who comes to the house for two hours per week and they spend time each evening and at weekends hearing him read and working on phonics with him.

Harry expresses himself well orally, using words which are very sophisticated and adult. His reading is improving (RA 8.4) but his handwriting and spelling are so poor that it is sometimes difficult to work out what he has written. He doesn't just confuse *b* and *d* but also *h* and *y*, *p* and *b*. Increasingly, he uses a small bank of words that he knows he can spell.

His parents want him to be withdrawn from French on the grounds that he has enough problems with English. The French teacher reports that Harry is doing well with his comprehension and spoken French and is one of the more able children in the class.

Some staff get exasperated with Harry as he is quite clumsy, seems to be in a dream half the time and cannot remember a simple sequence of instructions. He has difficulty telling left from right and so is often talking about the wrong diagram in a book or out of step in PE and sport. 'He's just not trying,' said one teacher, while others think he needs 'to grow up a bit'.

He is popular with the girls in his class and recently has made friends with some of the boys in the choir. Music is Harry's great passion but his parents are not willing for him to learn an instrument at the moment.

You will need to find out:

Specific strengths and weaknesses, both in general and within mathematics

Harry's strengths are the foundations upon which we can build his self-esteem in this subject. He may demonstrate some written language difficulties, and may not accurately read texts, instructions, or graphs charts and diagrams, and these difficulties will have an effect on his general mathematics capabilities. However, he may well have strengths in handling numbers, and have sound mental calculation skills, and it is therefore essential to find out what he can do in each of the areas of mathematics – Using and applying mathematics, Number and calculations, Algebra, Shape, space and measures and Handling data – and to what extent his specific difficulties hinder his understanding of any of these areas.

Standard written testing and examination procedures will inhibit Harry's capacity to demonstrate how he understands his mathematics. Oral assessment of Harry's work is therefore crucial, though time consuming (an accommodation with the TA for this task would enable the TA to undertake the oral assessment or release time for the teacher to do so). Furthermore, if teachers rely on written standard test scores to organise sets, then care must be taken that Harry is not placed in a set that may be inappropriate for his mathematical development, for this will have a serious and unnecessary impact on both his progress and his self-esteem.

How does Harry express himself?

At some stage, Harry will have to demonstrate his understanding both orally and in written form. The mathematics classroom should not be excluded from any writing strategies that are developed for Harry. These are likely to encourage the drafting process for any extended writing tasks, and therefore should include the use of ICT. The wordprocessor is a powerful tool for drafting and redrafting work – occasionally misused as a 'typing up' tool, but if Harry drafts his ideas directly using ICT, and is then encouraged to reread and redraft, either with TA support, or as part of a class exercise where children are recording their work in pairs or groups, then the quality of his reasoning and his use of mathematical vocabulary are enhanced alongside the development of his general under-standing of language.

Voice recognition software may be an alternative, effective way for Harry to present his reasoning, and alongside software that produces diagrams and charts (spreadsheets, dynamic geometry software (see below)), he will be able to produce good quality written reports.

There are alternatives to written recording, such as tapes or videos, through which Harry could express his work orally. This may be acceptable for homework tasks.

You should consider:

Harry's personal organisation

Teachers may be interpreting Harry's genuine difficulties with personal organisation as 'immaturity'. Being organised requires us to have a mental map of a sequence of instructions and an understanding of the consequences of our actions. Young children are inexperienced with the latter; children with specific learning difficulties may have genuine problems with both.

The approach to calculation: using mental calculation as a first resource

The NNS promotes this sequence of approaching calculations:

1 Children should use mental strategies as a first resort. They should always ask 'Can I do this in my head?'

2 Children should be encouraged to *use jottings to support mental calculations.*

3 Progress from expanded written methods to more compact written methods as and when children's understanding allows.

Developing mental arithmetic skills does not imply rote learning, e.g. multiplication facts. Kay and Yeo (2003) argue that 'it is simply not productive or appropriate for dyslexic learners to be required to learn the times table facts using the traditional rote-learning methods.' There are many ways in which an understanding of the times tables can be built through examining the structure of the number system, and children should be invited to reason about multiplication facts by examining links, e.g. How does 4×6 compare to 2×6, or 9×7 compare to 10×7?

Some strategies you/the TA could try:

Discussion, whole-class, structured lessons; group work

Opportunities must be created for Harry to develop his skills of reasoning, through discussion and group work. In this way, we are using his strength in self-expression and his own self-esteem will be raised, for he will have many opportunities to shine and have his understanding recognised through a medium that does not disadvantage him.

Given Harry's difficulties with both the written word *and* sequences of instructions, it is important that regular techniques are built up in the mathematics classroom for ensuring that children are clear about what they have to do. For this reason, the structured mathematics lesson has many benefits, where objectives and outcomes are made clear through discussion and children feel free to ask questions to clarify instructions.

Paired or group working will also help Harry to become involved in tasks, since through tackling the task together, children will be constantly revisiting the aims and the purpose of the task, and the sequence of instructions they have to follow will be regularly discussed. In this way, the chances of Harry 'losing his way' become minimised.

Our presentation

Work that we present to children should be clear, preferably printed from computers and large enough to be read comfortably.

Work on the board should not be cluttered; use colours effectively to emphasise main points.

The use of Key Vocabulary lists, specific for the series of lessons (Chapter 4) would benefit Harry greatly – he would have a ready reference for any written or oral work.

Using study skills – mind maps, association techniques, flow charts

Some children benefit from colour associations with various concepts. For instance, if Harry is encouraged to think of left as yellow and right as red, and reminders existed around the room (e.g. above the board, LEFT printed in yellow, RIGHT printed in red, or also in his own exercise book), these could trigger different ways of thinking and reduce confusion.

Associations can also be used in remembering instructions, for example if each line of instruction is associated with a different room in the house, then as Harry makes his journey through these rooms, he may remember the relevant instruction he is to follow. For example:

Kitchen – Draw a square.

Dining room – Find its area.

Living room – Find its perimeter.

Hall – Write down the results.

Stairs – Are the results the same number?

Back to kitchen – Draw another square.

Different visual representations of instructions may also help Harry, for example using the spider diagram technique, which is similar to mind-mapping (Chapter 5 and Appendix 5.3), but instead inserting a series of instructions. Similarly, the standard presentation of flow charts may be introduced as a technique for giving class instructions.

Other ICT packages

A variety of software should also be used to encourage oral work, and an understanding of fundamental mathematical concepts.

The ATM *Developing Number* software focuses on three elements: complements to 10, 100, 1000, 1 and 0.1, multiplication tables and place value. The last may be a problem for Harry, if he is misreading numbers. This part of the program has exercises to compare numbers written with words, with numbers expressed numerically or shown on a grid. The language of the place value is made explicit; the actual places are made explicit.

Dynamic geometry software packages (e.g. *Cabri, Geometer's Sketchpad*) are also valuable tools to help Harry overcome the physical constraints of his difficulty. He can set instructions, using properties of shapes, to create shapes and diagrams, and can explore properties such as symmetry or area quickly and without having to create lots of diagrams for himself. This will also develop Harry's reasoning skills, which will be essential for him to overcome some of his memory difficulties.

Megan, Year 10; Wheelchair user

Megan is very outgoing, loud and tough. Everybody knows when she is around! No one feels sorry for her – they wouldn't dare! Megan has spina bifida and needs a wheelchair and personal care as well as educational support. She has upset a number of the less experienced classroom assistants who find her a real pain. Some of the teachers like her because she is very sparky. If she likes a subject, she works hard – or at least she did until this year.

Megan has to be up very early for her parents to help get her ready for school before the bus comes at 7.50 am. She lives out of town and is one of the first to be picked up and one of the last to be dropped off so she has a longer school day than many of her classmates. Tiredness can be a problem as everything takes her so long to do and involves so much effort.

Now she is 15, she has started working towards her GCSEs and has the potential to get several A to Cs particularly in Maths and sciences. She is intelligent but is in danger of becoming disaffected because everything is so much harder for her than for other children. Recently she has lost her temper with a teacher, made cruel remarks to a very sensitive child and turned her wheelchair round so she sat with her back to a supply teacher. She has done no homework for the last few weeks saying that she doesn't see the point as 'no-one takes a crip seriously'.

You will need to find out:

Special arrangements for examinations

Consideration must be given at an early stage to the kind of support Megan may need for sitting her examinations. She may just need extra time, but if she is expected to use an amanuensis, or perhaps ICT (though this is not so likely for a mathematics exam), then the opportunities for these kinds of support must be built into the regular classroom practice, as well as for mock examinations. Megan should be invited to join in making these decisions, both about support and special examination arrangements.

You should consider:

Megan should be fully involved in decision-making

Any strategy for helping Megan must take account of raising her self-esteem. Her self-perception will be highly sensitive to the relationships she develops with everyone at school – teachers and TAs, pupils and other adults. It will also be affected by the extent to which she feels she has control or responsibility over her educational future. She must be fully involved in both decision-making and the formulation of strategies. For example, if she has difficulties in sustaining the effort for the full range of subjects, but is keen to attain the highest grades for her GCSE in certain areas, she should be invited to design her timetable, which may need to accommodate time at school for her to develop her coursework or homework assignments, possibly in a supportive setting (with a TA or teacher).

Appropriate grouping, managing support

In mathematics, it is hoped that she will be placed in the appropriate academic group first, and then any possibility of support explored after that. Schools often will have large groups for the most able pupils: Megan may find herself in a top set GCSE mathematics group, commonly with 30 or more pupils. This will present its own problems – physically accommodating this number of pupils in many classrooms is difficult enough, but care must here be taken that Megan has access both to the room itself and within it, and that she is also able to make a reasonable choice of where she is comfortable within the room. All these 'little' decisions add up to having an impact on her self-perception.

It is also unlikely that the top set GCSE mathematics group will enjoy the benefit of a TA to support Megan. Even if there were a TA, care should be taken as to how this TA actually works with her, and to what extent the TA can support Megan's mathematical development. Megan may not feel comfortable with a TA next to her all lesson; however, if the TA feels unable to support others in the group, whose needs are more likely to be help with the high-level mathematics, then the TA may be placed in a difficult situation. There may be a need for the teacher to call on help to develop specific diagrams or written pieces, which themselves would minimise Megan's physical effort of writing and drawing, but these may be prepared in advance. If there were room, and class sizes allowed it, two teachers working together with a larger group may offer better support for the whole class.

Some strategies you/the TA could try:

ICT

ICT can be used effectively to support Megan. Clearly, using graphic calculators, wordprocessors and spreadsheets can take some of the menial work out of calculations and drafting her work. Dynamic geometry software packages (e.g. *Cabri*, *Geometer's Sketchpad*) are valuable tools to help her overcome the physical constraints of her difficulty. She can set instructions, using properties of shapes, to create shapes and diagrams, and can explore properties such as symmetry or area quickly and without having to create lots of diagrams for herself.

Regular group work; differentiation by paired grouping

However, it is possible to consider physical support for Megan from another source. If the culture within the whole classroom is geared towards mutual support rather than individualised working, then Megan will have a much greater opportunity (as will all the pupils) of belonging to it. To develop this culture, activities designed for group work and discussion would enable the teacher to structure groups so that pupils help each other – both to understand the mathematics, any use of ICT and – as a natural part of the way the class works – with any physical support for drawing/writing that may be needed. Classrooms built around separate desks and individual silent work from textbooks deny the mutual support that arises from children discussing how to solve problems, as well as help with any physical drawing that may need doing.

Megan could also be considered an 'expert' in some groupings, rather than just the person who needs some help – she may be chosen to work with others because she has a particular skill or understanding in a specific area of mathematics. (Note McNamara and Moreton's (1997) discussion of differentiation.) The desks may need to be pushed together; the classroom may be a little noisier because children are talking about their mathematics rather than trying to solve problems in isolation, but children's handling of mathematical vocabulary, reasoning and problem-solving will all improve, and Megan will not have to feel different, because the whole class will be operating in a way that includes everyone.

Managing classroom discussion

There are more direct ways of raising self-esteem. Class discussions, where children are invited to explain their methods and reasoning (for instance in making calculations, or in representing or interpreting data) should be the norm. The teacher can then model these explanations on the board, and the class should be invited to compare and evaluate methods. This technique can help to overcome misconceptions, but if the classroom culture enables such open discussions to take place as part of general practice, then children develop a greater self-respect by realising that their ideas are acknowledged and respected by their peers.

The rules of this classroom apply to everyone. (Note 'A conjecturing atmosphere' illustrated in Chapter 4.) It works because it enables everyone to learn, and to be free both to succeed and to make mistakes, without ridicule. Megan's outgoing nature can be both positive and negative in effect. She may be inclined to dominate the class, but must be reminded why we take turns to listen to each other; she may find a great deal of support from this way of working, in that she will be ready to contribute, and will be rewarded with regular, positive feedback for her ideas.

Formative, peer and self-assessment

Finally, this class should certainly be developing their experience of assessing their own work. Chapter 6 illustrates some techniques for self- and peer assessment, and the use of pupil versions of GCSE MA1 criteria will be especially relevant (Appendix 6.6). Lesson objectives could be taken from the course specification, and pupils should be given regular opportunities to express their views on their progress.

If Megan finds herself belonging to a community that takes the views of all its pupils seriously, then she will have no cause to suggest that she is excluded from this. The examples of the way we work can be made explicit – listening to her self-assessment; using her expertise to help others in groups; the classroom atmosphere that respects the views of every pupil, through examining pupils' methods and reasoning; and the decisions about her timetable and support that she has made.

Steven, Year 8; Emotional and behavioural difficulties

'Stevie' is a real charmer – sometimes! He is totally inconsistent: one day, he is full of enthusiasm, the next day, he is very tricky and he needs to be kept on target. He thrives on attention. In primary school, he spent a lot of time sitting by the teacher's desk and seemed to enjoy feeling special. If he sat there he would get on with his work, but then as soon as he moved to sit with his friends he wanted to make sure he was the centre of attention.

Now in Year 8, Steven sometimes seems lazy – looking for the easy way out – but at other times he is quite dynamic and has lots of bright ideas. He can't work independently and has a very short attention span. No one has very high expectations of him and he is not about to prove them wrong.

Some of the children don't like him because he can be a bully, but really he is not nasty. He is a permanent lieutenant for some of the tougher boys and does things to win their approval.

He is a thief but mostly he takes silly things, designed to annoy rather than for any monetary value. He was found with someone's library ticket and stole one shoe from the changing rooms during PE.

Since his mother has begun a relationship with a new partner there has been a deterioration in behaviour and Steven has also been cautioned by police after stealing from a local DIY store. He has just been suspended for throwing a chair at a teacher, but staff suspect this was because he was on a dare. He certainly knows how to get attention.

You will need to find out:

Steven's interests and preferred learning styles

Steven clearly has a need to be the centre of attention, but this can be used to the advantage of the classroom. In finding out about Steven's interests and learning styles (as part of a process for the whole group), you can demonstrate that he belongs to an environment where all children's views and ways of learning are respected. These interests could then be used as contexts for mathematical problems, e.g. football could be used as the context for work on handling data; music in developing an understanding of patterns (leading to algebra). Furthermore, the interests could be used as part of the social well-being of the class (*'How did your team get on?' 'Have you learned to play that tune on the guitar yet?'*). These kinds of conversations need not be long, but can demonstrate the teacher's genuine interest in the pupils, giving a welcoming feeling to the class.

Steven's attention is more likely to be held in lessons where the ways of learning reflect his preferences (e.g. using physical mathematical equipment, or an emphasis on visual displays, such as using OHP equipment). Such materials may be all it takes to retain his attention so that he is not triggered into distracting behaviour.

You should consider:

Classroom culture

Although Steven's behaviour difficulties are more specific and possibly more extreme than others in the group, it is important to note that his poor behaviour is more likely to occur where there is general, low-level disruption in the class as a whole. For most pupils, classroom behaviour reflects the culture of the whole class: if they perceive that the usual practice is to undermine the lesson with disruptive, well-timed comments, then they will join in. Steven may initiate some of the problems because he may not have the necessary self-control, but you are far more likely to have successful lessons with him if he works in a classroom that is well managed, where the rules are clear for all, and where the general atmosphere is one of purposeful activity.

Body language, position

Sit down when working with Steven. Working at the same eye level is perceived as non-threatening. Steven will also read your facial expressions and your use of language carefully, and it is essential that you notice these aspects of your own behaviour as they are happening.

Some strategies you/the TA could try:

Plan for managing Steven's behaviour

In addition to planning the mathematics of the lesson, it is important to be prepared for dealing with any of the expected possible situations that may arise from Steven's behaviour. Prepare your own actions, how you will deal with a range of possible responses, and be clear about the school's structures for dealing with problems that can no longer reasonably be contained in the classroom.

Be calm

Steven's behaviour is not likely to be directed *at you*, but *from him*. There may appear to be no difference, but keeping the perspective that he does not intend to threaten may allow you to deal with issues objectively.

Be consistent

Mean what you say, do as you promise. Steven needs to trust the people who work with him, and we act as role models for positive behaviour.

Be clear

Explain Steven's choices for behaviour, and the consequences of those choices.

Build the working relationship; repair and rebuild

If you are able to support him in an extra-curricular activity – sport, drama or music workshop – the working relationship will have a chance to develop positively. A shared humour is also useful to encourage pupils to stay on task, and work with you, rather than against you.

If things go wrong – and you are human too – it is important for Steven to realise that there is no grudge, and that you both have a way back to get the working relationship together again. Make an opportunity to see Steven at times outside the classroom and perhaps arrange a meeting at registration, or break/lunchtime to discuss a problem in a calmer and less charged atmosphere. It is all too easy for the classroom to become an arena for conflict, so it is necessary to follow up issues away from it.

Create regular opportunities to praise

This can usually be achieved in the discussion episodes of the lesson – where carefully directed questions can lead to Steven giving answers that are useful for the class. These questions could be focused on the calculation methods that Steven uses, or on something that he has found in his work, or on an observation he has made. The TA could help the teacher identify aspects of his work worthy of praise. If appropriate, use the merit system that exists in the school to reward good work – whether oral or written contributions.

Structured, episodic mathematics lessons, use a range of resources

Thinking of a structure to the lesson that has a series of episodes can help pupils who have difficulties in sustaining concentration for long periods of time. Different activities, based on the same or linked objectives, enable children to gain different perspectives of the same ideas – developing their understanding further. Different presentations, especially using ICT, and interactive whiteboards can be powerful tools for focusing attention.

Maintain high expectations, demonstrate achievement through effective use of assessment

It is easy to fall into the trap of offering low-level, easy work that does not challenge pupils with behavioural difficulties, but this creates a negative cycle of low achievement and low self-esteem, leading to more poor behaviour. The work may appear to keep them quiet for a while, but they will know that they are not being challenged, and will feel the school is not offering them something worthwhile.

Most children will respond positively when they recognise that they are achieving, and the use of formative assessment (Chapter 6) coupled with activities appropriate for the age group (as indicated by the *Framework for Teaching Mathematics: Years 7, 8 and 9*, DfES 2001) will ensure that expectations are kept high.

Matthew, Year 9; Cognitive and learning difficulties

Matt is a very passive boy. He has no curiosity, no strong likes or dislikes. One teacher said, 'He's the sort of boy who says yes to everything to avoid further discussion but I sometimes wonder if he understands anything'.

Now in Year 9, he is quite a loner. He knows all the children and does not feel uncomfortable with them but is always on the margins. Often in class he sits and does nothing, just stares into space. He is no trouble and indeed if there is any kind of conflict, he absents himself or ignores it. No one knows very much about him as he never volunteers any information. In French, he once said that he had a dog, and one teacher has seen him on the local common with a terrier but no one is sure if it is his.

He does every piece of work as quickly as possible to get it over with. His work is messy and there is no substance to anything he does which makes it hard for teachers to suggest a way forward, or indeed to find anything to praise. Matthew often looks a bit grubby and is usually untidy. He can be quite clumsy and loses things regularly but does not bother to look for them. He does less than the minimum.

He is in a low set for maths but stays in the middle. He has problems with most humanities subjects because he has no empathy and no real sense of what is required. When the class went to visit a museum for their work on the Civil War, he was completely unmoved. To him, it was just another building and he could not really link it with the work they had done in history.

You will need to find out:

Matthew's interests and learning styles

Taking an interest in Matthew will at least give him an experience of being at the centre, help to develop his expressive skills, and then his own interests can be used as effective contexts for problem-solving, where this is appropriate. Discussion with parents should reveal what he does at home, and may lead to extending his home activities.

Ask Matthew about the type of work he likes to do, and if he prefers to see information in visual, written or physical forms, to determine his preferred learning style. Matthew is more likely to respond to work if it is in a form that facilitates his learning. Activities could be designed accordingly, to enhance his motivation.

Diagnostic information about Matthew's mathematical capabilities

Identify Matthew's strengths and weaknesses in the various mathematical areas. It is likely that Matthew has:

- poor understanding of basic mathematical ideas, such as the mathematical meaning of 'difference' or operations like division;

- limited understanding of mathematical vocabulary;

- poor communication skills;

- problems with logical reasoning;

- difficulty with problem-solving – applying knowledge to new situations.

Wider learning difficulties

Find out information about Matthew's literacy (e.g. reading age, spelling age), internal examination performance and SAT scores.

You should consider:

Additional difficulties

Matthew may also experience some specific learning difficulties, as exemplified by his poor personal organisation, and the weak presentation of his work.

Matthew may also experience dyspraxia, which will have an effect on his motor and language skills, and he may, therefore, need specific support in handling mathematical equipment.

Matthew may also have problems with auditory or visual memory. This will mean that he forgets instructions, and is off task quite regularly.

Matthew's self-esteem

This is not likely to be high. Matthew will be well aware of his difficulties, but his survival technique of avoiding the task will not contribute to any feelings of success. If his work is so limited that it is 'difficult to praise', then situations must be engineered where he does receive – and enjoy – praise. These situations are most likely to arise in the oral interactions he has with the teacher and TA, initially, and later, when working relationships are established, with his peers.

Some strategies you/the TA could try:

Develop Matthew's oral skills – reasoning, explaining, listening and working in groups

The teacher and TA will need to plan together how this could be achieved. Matthew's greatest difficulties need to be addressed – how he communicates and relates to others, and his powers of reasoning are directly related. Individualised book work will not address these – setting up situations where groups or pairs work together on solving a problem will begin to tackle Matthew's social difficulties and help him to engage more effectively with the work. The group will have to be monitored by the TA or teacher and occasionally led by one of them to model the desired ways of working. If Matthew has problems with staying on task, it is more likely that this will be overcome when a group has been given a shared task, and there is regular reaffirmation of the task and his role in completing it.

In problem-solving activities, Matthew must be given opportunities to explain how he tackles calculations, and identify any patterns or observations he has made. These opportunities may be in the pairs, with a TA or with the whole group.

Lesson or topic vocabulary (a short list placed at the front of the class) will support Matthew's explanations. Refer to it regularly through the lessons, and invite children to use some of the words as they discuss their ideas.

Developing an understanding of mathematical processes, structuring writing

Some processes can be structured, e.g. a problem-solving process can be unpicked into simpler steps, guiding children through solving. Appendix 5.4 can be used both for structuring a way of working, and as a writing frame for the work. The data handling process (see Chapter 4) can be structured for children in a similar way.

ICT

Matthew's self-esteem may be enhanced when he produces work of a reasonable quality, and the use of wordprocessors, spreadsheets and dynamic geometry software facilitate this process of drafting and re-editing to produce text, diagrams and charts. The drafting process takes some effort, which Matthew does not demonstrate, and so he will need regular monitoring, TA/teacher support or paired work to ensure that a task is completed.

Monitor Matthew's use of mathematical equipment carefully

If Matthew displays clumsiness, he will find great difficulties in handling precision mathematical equipment such as a protractor, pair of compasses, pencil and ruler. Other specialised equipment (Cuisenaire, interlocking cubes) may also present physical difficulties, leading to frustration if appropriate support is not given.

Structured lessons; oral and mental starters

Matthew will respond more effectively to lessons organised into shorter episodes, where the outcomes of the tasks are made explicit and are achievable. Lesson starters could be used as regular practice for calculation skills, developing vocabulary and working with units of measurement, e.g. using timetables, converting between units.

Bhavini, Year 9; Visual impairment

Bhavini has very little useful sight. She uses a stick to get around school and some of the other children make cruel comments about this which she finds very hurtful. She also wears glasses with thick lenses which she hates. On more than one occasion, she has been knocked over in the corridor but she insists that these incidents were accidents and that she is not being bullied. However, her sight is so poor she may not recognise pupils who pick on her.

She has a certain amount of specialist equipment such as talking scales in food technology and a CCTV for textbooks, but now in year 9, she is always conscious of being different. Her classmates accept her but she is very cut off as she does not make eye contact or see well enough to find people she knows to sit with at break. She spends a lot of time hanging around the support area. Her form tutor has tried to get other children to take her under their wing or to escort her to Humanities, which is in another building, but this has bred resentment. She has friends outside school at the local Phab club (Physically handicapped/able bodied) and has taken part in regional VI Athletics tournaments, although she opts out of sport at school if she can. Some of the teachers are concerned about health and safety issues and there has been talk about her being disapplied from Science.

She has a reading age approximately three years behind her chronological age and spells phonetically. Many of the teaching strategies used to make learning more interesting, tend to disadvantage her. The lively layout of her French book with cartoons and speech bubbles is a nightmare. Even if she has a page on her CCTV or has a photocopy of the text enlarged she cannot track which bit goes where. At the end of one term she turned up at the support base asking for some work to do because, 'They're all watching videos'.

You will need to find out:

School strategies for receiving and presenting visual information
The school may develop alternative strategies for presentation, e.g. audiotapes, ICT or any other specialised equipment.

Bhavini's mathematical capabilities
Bhavini's reading difficulties are not severe, but may have had an effect on her understanding of some mathematical language, and therefore her understanding of mathematical concepts – especially in Data handling, Shape, space and measures, and in solving written problems.

Arrangements for moving about school
Bhavini may be given more time to move from one classroom to another, and may therefore leave classrooms early. Alternatively, a pupil in the class may have responsibility for helping her.

Appropriate lighting for Bhavini's working environment

Bhavini may be affected by bright lights, or by an environment that is too dark. It may be necessary for Bhavini to work in a particular area of a particular room, and have most of her lessons there.

Printed text

From the SENCO, find out exactly what Bhavini *can* see, and how materials should be presented. For example, she may be able to read a certain sized print, and certain types of font are likely to be preferable, e.g. clear fonts such as Arial, with certain types of spacing, as in Figure 8.1.

Arial size 16 point, **16 point bold**
Arial size 24 point, **24 point bold**

Figure 8.1 *Illustrating different sizes of font*

If there are possibilities with printed text, then you must ensure that she has her own specially printed copies of the relevant material, but it must be kept to a minimum, clear and uncluttered.

Colours

Find out if using colour could be a useful source of support for Bhavini. Colours can be used effectively to clarify or emphasise, with specific sections of text highlighted in advance, or indicating different parts of a diagram or angles on a drawing. This strategy has the aim of clarifying, rather than 'making learning interesting'.

You should consider:

Producing written work

Wordprocessing software set up to produce text with Bhavini's preferred font; size and any colour requirements could be used in class.

Voice recognition software may be an alternative, effective way for Bhavini to present her reasoning, and alongside software that produces diagrams and charts (spreadsheets, dynamic geometry software (see 'Harry' in this chapter)), she will be able to produce good quality written reports. A group could complete these reports – other pupils could contribute by using the same software as Bhavini.

However, it is important to recognise our values here: to what extent is learning achieved primarily through written activities? Is there a need for much of the work to be written? Evidence for learning can be clearly demonstrated through actions, the spoken word, and through mathematical constructions. These are outlined in the sections on kinaesthetic, auditory and visual learning in Chapter 5.

Group/paired work

Bhavini will benefit greatly from working in a classroom where group/paired work is a strength. If the whole class is used to this way of working, there will be regular changes to the structure of the groups, and clearly defined roles for each member of the group. As there is no indication that Bhavini has difficulties with mathematical concepts, she can be given opportunities to be the 'expert' in a particular aspect of mathematics, so that she may help others. In return, the work in presenting ideas or translating visual information into auditory information can be shared.

Lighting, positioning

Bhavini should work in an appropriately lit environment, and you should not stand in silhouette against the window or other backlit source when addressing her. Glare from whiteboards or interactive whiteboards must be addressed when selecting her place in the classroom.

Some strategies you/the TA could try:

Questioning, discussion

Begin questions with Bhavini's name, so that you are sure you have her attention. Draw her attention carefully to any part of the board, display or poster that is being discussed. She may not notice slight facial or hand gestures, so instructions will need to be verbally clear.

Oral work

It is likely that Bhavini can contribute ably to any oral episode of structured mathematics lessons. Ensure that she has many opportunities to develop her understanding of mathematical concepts in this way, as the written form will inevitably be slower for her.

Personal organisation, easy access to mathematical equipment

It is important for Bhavini to organise herself so that she can easily find any books, rulers, pencils and pens that she brings to class. Alternatively, she may be helped with a personal tray or cupboard space in the classroom. Any mathematical equipment should be clearly labelled, so that she may get it for herself if possible, to encourage her own independence.

Use of mathematical tools and equipment with tactile qualities

Some mathematical materials still hold value for visually impaired pupils, as they also have tactile qualities, for example:

- **Cuisenaire rods** – for comparison of lengths/numbers; factors, fractions, decimals, ratio, percentages and some work on algebra. These are designed with different lengths and colours, but even if difficulties remain, a set of these rods could be adapted by drilling the appropriate number of holes through them, so that they can be recognised through touch.

- **Interlocking cubes** – for work on areas and volumes; enlargement of shapes, algebra (forming patterns and sequences). Large cubes are also available.

- **Shape-building materials** (e.g. *Geostrips* (Invicta)/*Polydron*) – for identifying and creating shapes and exploring their properties.

- **ATM mats** – tessellation, building regular solids, finding areas and perimeters of rectangles and squares.

- **Taktiles** (*Algebra through Geometry* (G. Giles/Tarquin) – to explore areas of shapes and express these areas algebraically;

- **Probability equipment** – dice/coins/shakers with numbered counters – to explore experimental probability and compare with theoretical probability. Again, large dice and counters are also available for this work.

- **Diene's blocks, place value (arrow) cards** – to explore place value in numbers. These have tactile qualities to reinforce ideas of place value.

Use of other mathematical tools and equipment

- Some tools will present their own difficulties. Protractors and rulers, measuring jugs and scales using small calibrations will be impossible for Bhavini to read.

- It may be possible for Bhavini to read rulers with 1 cm divisions, but not millimetre divisions. Her understanding of measuring length can be enhanced through approximating lengths, e.g. to the nearest cm, or she may be invited to estimate lengths to nearest millimetres, having her estimations confirmed by another pupil or TA.

- In the same way, she may be able to read a protractor marked at every 10°, and estimate angles in between.

- Angles software, such as *SMILE* 90° or 360°, where children are asked to estimate angles, or dynamic geometry software (*Cabri, Geometer's Sketchpad*) both create and measure angles of certain sizes. *Logo* is also a powerful software for understanding angle.

- As a kinaesthetic activity, try having the class stand up and turn through certain angles or bearings (having found north first).

Changing the media for learning – kinaesthetic activities, auditory activities, visualisation tasks

Chapter 5 explores some of the activities that may be useful to consider. Developing Bhavini's skills at personal visualisation will also be useful, e.g. translating a text that is read to the class into pictures.

Susan, Year 10; Complex difficulties, Autistic Spectrum Disorder

Susan is a tall, very attractive girl who has been variously labelled as having Aspergers' and 'cocktail party syndrome'. She talks fluently but usually about something totally irrelevant. She is very charming and her language is sometimes quite sophisticated but her ability to use language for school work in Year 10 operates at a much lower level. Her reading is excellent on some levels but she cannot draw inferences from the printed word. If you ask her questions about what she has read, she looks blank, echoes what you have said, looks puzzled or changes the subject – something she is very good at.

She finds relationships quite difficult. She is very popular, especially with the boys in her class. They think she is a laugh. There have been one or two problems with some of the boys in school. Her habit of standing too close to people and her over-familiarity have led to misunderstandings which have upset her. Her best friend Laura is very protective of her and tries to mother her, to the extent of doing some of her work for her so she won't get into trouble.

Her work is limited. In art all her pictures look the same – very small, cramped drawings – and she does not like to use paint because, 'it's messy'. She finds it very hard to relate to the wider world and sees everything in terms of her own experience. The class has been studying *Macbeth* and she has not moved beyond saying, 'I don't believe in witches and ghosts'.

Some teachers think she is being wilfully stupid or not paying attention. She seems to be attention-seeking as she is very poor at turn- taking and shouts out in class if she thinks of something to say or wants to know how to spell a word. When she was younger, she used to retreat under the desk when she was upset and had to be coaxed out. She is still easily offended and cannot bear being teased. She has an answer for everything and while it may not be sensible or reasonable, there is an underlying logic.

You will need to find out:

What does Susan understand in mathematics?

If Susan has some difficulty with drawing inferences from the written word, or difficulties with interpreting text, then it is very likely she will have difficulties in solving word problems. She may be fluent in some mathematical skills, where she is competent with handling procedures to make calculations, but she may not know *when* to apply particular skills. Offering a range of contexts for similar problems, and then helping her to identify the similarities between the problems will help her to apply her skills more effectively.

Understand how she relates to you

She may not offer eye contact – it should not be expected. Her ways of relating to you may appear odd, e.g. she may keep an inappropriate physical space or her conversation may not match either the topic or the audience.

How much does Susan need individual space in which to work?

Susan may need a quiet, undisturbed area in which to work. She may be more productive if she is allowed to work on her own. Of course, she will need to be supervised carefully, and helped when required.

Find out if lighting or noise affect her, and modify the classroom accordingly.

You should consider:

Understanding of mathematical language

Some children with autism have a special creative or mathematical skill (about 10 per cent), but many will display difficulties with social interaction, communication and the development of imagination. These difficulties will affect mathematical development – the language of mathematics is accurate and complex, and understanding specific vocabulary will present challenges, especially where mathematical words have different meanings in common usage, e.g. 'property', 'operation', 'net'. There may also be difficulties where related meanings are illustrated precisely, but a small difference exists – such as where vertical and horizontal are perpendicular to each other, but not all perpendicular pairs of lines are vertical and horizontal.

Susan's needs for routine

A clear timetable and regular areas for working need to be set out for Susan. It may also be useful for her to have clear, visual references – timetables, and labels for materials will support her in the school.

This need will also be addressed through structuring the mathematics lessons carefully, and clarifying the objectives and outcomes required of her.

Some strategies you/the TA could try:

Your approach to Susan

- Be calm, patient, adaptable.

- Be positive, and have high expectations.

- Refer to Susan directly, even when speaking to her as part of a group.

- Be explicit about positive social behaviour, e.g. taking turns, listening to others and responding to the views of other pupils.

- Offer clear guidance for behaviour, and when needed disapprove of the *behaviour,* not Susan.

- Despite her difficulties with jokes or humour, try to build these into your relationship with her – often 'running' jokes can be understood.

Development of language

Susan will find a mathematics dictionary, or a glossary of terms (e.g. that produced by QCA) very useful in helping her learn precise meanings for mathematical terms. Vocabulary lists – especially specific lesson vocabulary – will help Susan focus on key words being used in the lesson.

Writing frames, including structured 'problem-solving' frames (e.g. Appendix 5.4) will support both Susan's pattern of working and her use of language in explaining her thinking.

Working in groups/pairs; using a TA

Susan's popularity may have emerged from inappropriate behaviour, perhaps an unfortunate use of language or her lack of appreciation of personal space. It is possible that the boys who think she's a laugh may encourage her to entertain them in classroom group situations. Furthermore, her friend Laura appears over-protective, but her actions in completing work for Susan end up being unhelpful. In each of these situations, Susan is not in control of her part in these relationships but is becoming increasingly disempowered by them. As a result, it is essential to:

- Choose pairings/groups carefully – Susan should have opportunities to work with pupils who will help her to stay focused on task, who can help her and whom she can help with her own mathematical abilities.

- Give clear guidelines as to what is expected of any collaboration, including defining the roles of each member of the group.

- Monitor the work of the group.

- Ask the TA to work with the group, modelling the expected behaviour.

The TA could also help Susan by listening to her ideas and helping her modify them as a preparation to any class discussion on a particular topic. This process will help Susan to refine her statements, both orally and in writing if necessary. As a result, she will learn how to improve on the language she uses to express herself, and the extra stage of thinking will help her develop the quality of her ideas.

Jenny, Year 7; Down's Syndrome

Jenny is in Year 7 and has Down's syndome. She is a very confident child who has been cherished and encouraged by her mother and older brothers and sisters. She is very assertive and is more than capable of dealing with spiteful comments: 'I don't like it when you call me names. You're cruel and I hate you', but this assertiveness can lead to obstinacy. She is prone to telling teachers that they are wrong!

She has average skills in reading and writing but her work tends to be unimaginative and pedestrian. She enjoys biology but finds the rest of the science curriculum hard going. She has started to put on weight and tries to avoid PE. She has persuaded her mother to provide a note saying that she tires easily but staff know that she is a bundle of energy and is an active member of an amateur theatre group which performs musicals. She has a good singing voice and enjoys dancing.

She went to a local nursery and primary school and fitted in well. She always had someone to sit next to and was invited to all the best birthday parties. Teachers and other parents frequently praised her and she felt special.

Now in secondary school, everything has changed. Some of her friends from primary school have made new friendships and don't want to spend so much time with her. She is very hurt by this and feels excluded. She is also struck by how glamorous some of the older girls look and this has made her more self-conscious.

You will need to find out:

- The views of parents and the child herself, about what has been achieved and what are reasonable goals to achieve in the mathematics curriculum.

- Strategies being applied over the whole school, to ensure a consistent approach, in terms of managing behaviour as well as learning.

- How to listen to Jenny, if her pronunciation is not clear.

- The difference between 'can't do' and 'won't do'. Tasks will need to be carefully designed so that Jenny understands what to do – not too hard, too easy or too long.

You should consider:

Some general characteristics associated with Down's Syndrome have a specific bearing on the child's mathematical development, notably:

- difficulties with thinking and reasoning, and applying knowledge to new situations

- sequencing difficulties

These difficulties can have a severe effect on the child's understanding of number, even to the point of consistent one-to-one matching when counting. Jenny may therefore experience many difficulties with mathematical ideas. Lorenz (1998) conducted research of 25 secondary-aged children with Down's Syndrome in mainstream schools, the most able of whom were working at level 3 throughout KS3 and KS4. Similar results were shown by Buckley and Bird (1993).

There are associated behaviour problems, including a resistance to co-operate or undertake a task. Behaviour can change with effective management, and poor behaviour should not be accepted. Again, this aspect should be discussed with Jenny and her parents.

Too much one-to-one support can be counter-productive; Jenny should be given opportunities to work with other pupils who can provide positive models of behaviour and working. It may therefore not be appropriate for Jenny to work in a group where behaviour is already a problem.

The teacher must ensure regular contact with Jenny, to determine progress and effective planning.

Some strategies you/the TA could try:

Use mathematical equipment as the basis for activities

Use a range of mathematical equipment to develop visual imagery to reinforce mathematical ideas, develop reasoning from concrete situations and to promote discussion:

- **Cuisenaire rods** – for comparison of lengths/numbers; factors, fractions, decimals, ratio, percentages and some work on algebra;

- **Interlocking cubes** – for work on areas and volumes; enlargement of shapes, algebra (forming patterns and sequences);

- **Shape-building materials** (*Geostrips, Polydron*) – for identifying and creating shapes and exploring their properties;

- **ATM mats** – tessellation, building regular solids, finding areas and perimeters of rectangles and squares;

- **Taktiles** (*Algebra through Geometry* (G. Giles/Tarquin) to explore areas of shapes and express these areas algebraically;

- **Probability equipment** – dice/coins/shakers with numbered counters – to explore experimental probability and compare with theoretical probability;

- **Diene's blocks, place value (arrow) cards** – to explore place value in numbers.

Note, however, that Jenny may have difficulties with her motor skills, and some frustrations may occur when using these materials. Always monitor her progress in this respect carefully.

Use Jenny's visual strengths

Visual resources, such as number lines and counting sticks, mind maps/spider diagrams (Chapter 5) can help the child in counting (forwards and backwards), and help develop an understanding of addition and subtraction. Other aspects of mathematics can be supported visually, e.g. a compass rose (Appendices 8.1 and 8.2) for estimating or seeing the sequence in angles.

Structure progression carefully

The number line allows for careful progression in the four rules of number. As a supporting visual tool it would be particularly useful for Jenny, as it again works with her likely strength in handling visual information. Chapter 5 details this progression.

The *Mathsteps* assessment and teaching programme from Learning Development Aids (LDA) develops an understanding through finely graded steps and covers classification, numbers, sequences, space and shape, time, money, fractions, charts and volume.

Group/pair effectively

Establish a pattern of group or paired activities, to develop oral skills and co-operation. It may be useful to consider paired work with a child of weaker literacy skills, so that the partnership is mutually supportive, and so that Jenny can be the expert in reporting findings and expressing ideas. Many children with Down's Syndrome experience poor auditory memory, and verbal instructions may quickly be forgotten. Working in groups can help overcome this difficulty, but it may also be helpful to have instructions written clearly as a reminder.

Questioning and instructions

Always allow good time for a response to questions. Develop vocabulary carefully, reinforcing familiar terms regularly. The use of lesson vocabulary lists (Chapter 4) will help with this.

Instructions should be kept short and simple, and tasks should be repeated regularly so that the child can use the techniques in increasingly varied situations.

Appendices

An example of a departmental policy

General statement with reference to the school's special educational needs policy

All members of the department will ensure that the needs of all pupils with SEN are met, according to the aims of the school and its SEN policy.

Definition of SEN

Cognition and Learning Needs	Behavioural, Emotional and Social Development Needs	Communication and Interaction Needs	Sensory and/or Physical Needs
Specific learning difficulties (SpLD)	Behavioural, emotional and social difficulties (BESD)	Speech, language and communication needs	Hearing impairment (HI)
Dyslexia			Visual impairment (VI)
Moderate learning difficulties (MLD)	Attention Deficit Disorder (ADD)	Autistic Spectrum Disorder (ASD)	
Severe learning difficulties (SLD)	Attention Deficit Hyperactivity Disorder (ADHD)	Asperger's Syndrome	Multi-sensory impairment (MSI)
			Physical difficulties (PD)
Profound and multiple learning difficulties (PMLD)			Other

Provision for staff within the department

Members of staff with responsibility for overseeing the provision of SEN within the department will attend liaison meetings and feed back to other members of the department. They will maintain the department's SEN information file, attend appropriate training and disseminate this to all departmental staff. All information will be treated with confidentiality.

Provision for pupils with SEN

The pupils are grouped according to ability as informed by Key Stage 2 results, reading scores and any other relevant performance, social or medical information.

It is understood that pupils with SEN may receive additional support if they have a statement of SEN, or are at School Action or School Action Plus. The staff in the mathematics department will aim to support the pupils to achieve their targets as specified on their IEPs and will provide feedback for IEP or statement reviews. Pupils with SEN will be included in the departmental monitoring system used for all pupils. Additional support will be requested as appropriate.

Resources and learning materials

The department will provide suitably differentiated materials and, where appropriate, specialist resources for pupils with SEN. Additional texts are available for those pupils working below National Curriculum level 3. At Key Stage 4 an alternative course to GCSE is offered at Entry level, but where possible, pupils with SEN will be encouraged to reach their full potential and follow a GCSE course. Support staff will be provided with curriculum information in advance of lessons and will also be involved in lesson planning. A list of resources is available in the department handbook and on the notice board.

Staff qualifications and Continuing Professional Development needs

A record of training undertaken, specialist skills and training required will be kept in the department handbook. Requests for training will be considered in line with the department and school improvement plan.

Monitoring and reviewing the policy

The department SEN policy will be monitored by the head of department on a planned annual basis, with advice being sought from the SENCO as part of a three-yearly review process.

Activity: What do we really think?

Each member of the department should choose two of these statements and pin them on to the noticeboard for an overview of staff opinion. The person leading the session (Head of Department, SENCO, senior manager) should be ready to address any negative feedback and take forward the department in a positive approach.

If my own child had special needs, I would want her/him to be in a mainstream school mixing with all sorts of kids.

I want to be able to cater for pupils with SEN but feel that I don't have the expertise required.

Special needs kids in mainstream schools are all right up to a point, but I didn't sign up for dealing with the more severe problems – they should be in special schools.

It is the SENCO's responsibility to look out for these pupils with SEN – with help from support teachers.

Pupils with special needs should be catered for the same as any others. Teachers can't pick and choose the pupils they want to teach.

I need much more time to plan if pupils with SEN are going to be coming to my lessons.

Big schools are just not the right places for blind or deaf kids, or those in wheelchairs.

I would welcome more training on how to provide for pupils with SEN in mathematics.

I have enough to do without worrying about kids who can't read or write.

If their behaviour distracts other pupils in any way, youngsters with SEN should be withdrawn from the class.

SEN and Disability Act 2001 (SENDA)

1 The SEN and Disability Act 2001 amends the Disability Discrimination Act 1995 to include schools and LEAs responsibility to provide for pupils and students with disabilities.

2 The definition of a disability in this Act is:
'someone who has a physical or mental impairment that has an effect on his or her ability to carry out normal day to day activities. The effect must be:
- substantial (that is more than minor or trivial): and
- long term (that is, has lasted or is likely to last for at least a year or for the rest of the life of the person affected): and
- adverse.'

Activity: List any pupils that you come across that would fall into this category.

3 The Act states that the responsible body for a school must take such steps as it is reasonable to take to ensure that disabled pupils and disabled prospective pupils are not placed at substantial disadvantage in comparison with those who are not disabled.

Activity: Give an example of something which might be considered 'a substantial disadvantage'.

4 The duty on the school is to make reasonable adjustments is anticipatory. This means that a school should not wait until a disabled pupil seeks admission to consider what adjustments it might make generally to meet the needs of disabled pupils.

Activity: Think of two reasonable adjustments that could be made in your school/department.

5 The school has a duty to plan strategically for increasing access to the school education, this includes provision of information for pupils and parents (e.g. Braille or taped versions of brochures) improving the physical environment for disabled students and increasing access to the curriculum by further differentiation.

Activity: Consider ways of increasing access to the school for a pupil requesting admission who has Down's Syndrome with low levels of literacy and a heart condition that affects strenuous physical activity.

6 Schools need to be proactive in seeking out information about a pupil's disability (by establishing good relationships with parents and carers, asking about disabilities during admission interviews, etc.) and ensuring that all staff who might come across the pupil are aware of the pupil's disability.

Activity: List the opportunities that occur in your school for staff to gain information about disabled students. How can these be improved on?

Categories of SEN

Special Educational Need	Characteristics	Strategies
Attention Deficit Disorder – with or without hyperactivity	• has difficulty following instructions and completing tasks • easily distracted by noise, movement of others, attracting attention, objects • can't stop talking, interrupts others, calls out • acts impulsively without thinking about the consequences	• keep instructions simple – the one sentence rule • make eye contact and use the pupil's name when speaking to him • sit the pupil away from obvious distractions • provide clear routines and rules, rehearse them regularly
Autistic Spectrum Disorder	• may experience high levels of stress and anxiety when routines are changed • may have a literal understanding of language • more often interested in objects rather than people • may be sensitive to light, sound, touch or smell	• give a timetable for each day • warn the pupil about changes to usual routine • avoid using too much eye contact as it can cause distress • use simple clear language avoid using metaphor, sarcasm
Down's Syndrome	• takes longer to learn and consolidate new skills • limited concentration • has difficulties with thinking, reasoning, sequencing • has better social than academic skills • may have some sight, hearing, respiratory and heart problems	• use simple familiar language • give time for information to be processed • break lesson up into a series of shorter, varied tasks • accept a variety of ways of recording work, drawings, diagrams, photos, video

Special Educational Need	Characteristics	Strategies
Hearing Impairment	• hearing in right ear only • has a monaural loss	• check on the best seating position • check that the pupil can see your face for expressions and lip reading • indicate where a pupil is speaking from during class discussion, only allow one speaker at a time
Dyscalculia	• has a discrepancy between development level and general ability in maths • has difficulty counting by rote • misses out or reverses numbers • has difficulty with directions, left and right • loses track of turns in games, dance	• provide visual aids, number lines, lists of rules, formulae, words • encourage working out on paper • provide practical objects to aid learning

Instructions for activity

This activity should only take about 10 minutes but can be used for additional discussion on strategies, concentrating on the easy ones to implement or the ones already being used.

1. Photocopy onto paper or card.

2. Cut the first column off the sheet.

3. Cut out the remaining boxes.

4. Either keep the two sets of boxes separate, firstly matching the characteristics then the strategies, or use all together.

Alternative activity

Make the boxes bigger with room for additional strategies or remove a couple of the strategies so staff can add any they have used or can identify.

Using the number line

For fractions of quantities:

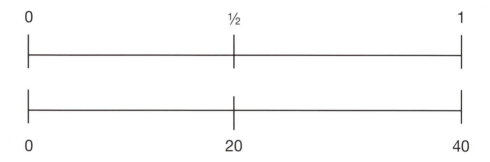

For comparing fractions, decimals and percentages:

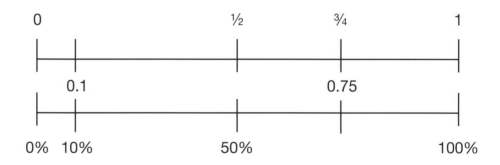

Planning sheet

Topic/unit/term Where this fits into the series of lessons		
Mental/oral starter		
Main activity	Objectives/the learning to be achieved/and why	
	Resources	
	Role of TA	
	Possible pupil difficulties	
Plenary	Key questions	
	Applying understanding (a problem based on the learning from the lesson)	
Homework		
Evaluation	Teacher	
	TA	

The front of the classroom

The number line

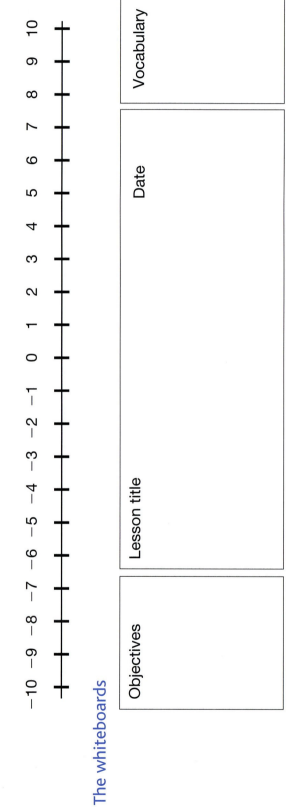

−10 −9 −8 −7 −6 −5 −4 −3 −2 −1 0 1 2 3 4 5 6 7 8 9 10

The whiteboards

Objectives	Lesson title	Date	Vocabulary

Posters/displays for the classroom

Number lines – Fractions, decimals and percentages

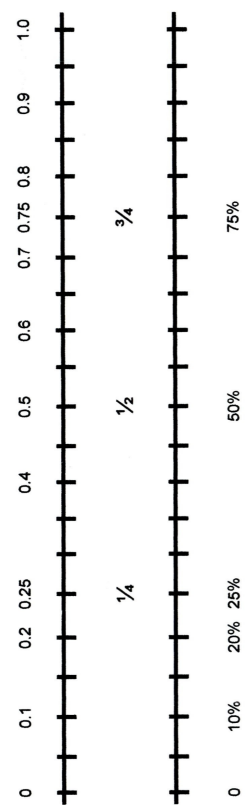

Using colour can highlight patterns. Not all the numbers should be inserted – this can be used as a teaching tool, for children to develop an understanding of the patterns and links in the number systems being used here. Children should be invited to predict other points on the number line (even beyond the 1.0 or 100% shown here) and justify and check their predictions.

Showing the links between place value column headings, powers, fractions, decimals and metric units

HTU – Place Value – Powers – Metric Units

M	HTh	TTh	Th	H	T	U	.	t	h	th	tth	hth	mth
Million	Hundred thousand	Ten thousand	Thousand	Hundred	Ten	Unit	point	Tenth	Hundredth	Thousandth	Ten thousandth	Hundred thousandth	Millionth
		10x10x10		10x10				$\frac{1}{10}$	$\frac{1}{(10\times10)}$				
			10^3							10^{-3}			
			1000				.	$^1/_{10}$	$^1/_{100}$				
			km			m	.		cm	mm			
						l	.		cl				
			kg			g				mg			

→ ÷10

→ x10

Can you complete the diagram? What links each row?

What is similar about the Thousand and the Thousandths columns? Are the same kinds of similarities in other pairs of columns?

If we divide or multiply by 10 to move to the next column, what do we multiply or divide by when moving across two columns? Three columns?

Times table charts

Table	×1	×2	×3	×4	×5	×6	×7	×8	×9	×10	×	×	×

The above blank may be used in a number of ways, again to illustrate links and patterns to help children understand the number system, e.g.:

Table	×1	×2	×3	×4	×5	×6	×7	×8	×9	×10	×	×	×
2	2	4	6		10		14						
0.2	0.2	0.4					1.4						
20	20	40			100								

(may be purchased from 'Education Initiatives' – see Appendix 4.14)

Further examples of making explicit links with number sequences

Table	×1	×2	×3	×4	×5	×6	×7	×8	×9	×10	×	×	×
¼	¼	½	¾	1									
½	½	1	1½	2	2½	3	3½						
¾	¾												

Table	×1	×2	×3	×4	×5	×6	×7	×8	×9	×10	×	×	×
2	2	4	6	8									
4	4	8	12	16									
8	6	16	24										

100 squares

This presentation of the number square reflects the popular language of 'going up in tens' and of numbers getting bigger.

91	92	93	94	95	96	97	98	99	100
81	82	83	84	85	86	87	88	89	90
71	72	73	74	75	76	77	78	79	80
61	62	63	64	65	66	67	68	69	70
51	52	53	54	55	56	57	58	59	60
41	42	43	44	45	46	47	48	49	50
31	32	33	34	35	36	37	38	39	40
21	22	23	24	25	26	27	28	29	30
11	12	13	14	15	16	17	18	19	20
1	2	3	4	5	6	7	8	9	10

1	2	3	4	5	6	7	8	9	10
11	12	13	14	15	16	17	18	19	20
21	22	23	24	25	26	27	28	29	30
31	32	33	34	35	36	37	38	39	40
41	42	43	44	45	46	47	48	49	50
51	52	53	54	55	56	57	58	59	60
61	62	63	64	65	66	67	68	69	70
71	72	73	74	75	76	77	78	79	80
81	82	83	84	85	86	87	88	89	90
91	92	93	94	95	96	97	98	99	100

Physical resources for the mathematics department

Number and calculations, including fractions, decimals and percentages. Many of these resources can be used for work in algebra.

Equipment	Some possible uses
Counting stick	Number sequences, tables
Number lines	For all four operations
Arrow cards	Demonstrating place value
Interlocking cubes	Number sequences, leading to algebra
Diene's blocks	Place value, relating numbers and decimals
Cuisenaire rods	Factors, fractions, decimals, percentages; algebra
ATM *Developing Number* software	Place value, tables, complements
Target boards	Calculations
OHT numbers	
OHT fractions circles, square grids (Learning Resources)	Recognising fractions, and calculating with them
Calculators – all types, including scientific, graphic	Comparing calculators reveals the need for the order of operations; calculator skills need to be explicitly taught
OHT thermometer	Negative and positive numbers
ICT – spreadsheet	Extended calculations, presentation of data
Money	Money and decimals
Fraction tiles/poster	Comparing relative sizes and equivalence of fractions

Algebra (see above – Cuisenaire, interlocking cubes, etc.)

Equipment	Some possible uses
Algebra through Geometry (G. Giles/Dime)	Expressing areas algebraically Collecting like terms
OHT co-ordinate grids	Graph drawing
Graph drawing software	

Shape, space and measures

Equipment	Some possible uses
ATM Shape Mats	Tessellations, geometric reasoning Making 3D shapes
Shape construction equipment (Polydron, Geostrips)	Construction, reasoning
Compasses, rulers, protractors, etc. There are also specialist resources for children with motor difficulties.	Construction, measurement
Paper – various mathematical papers	Construction, reasoning
Height measures – wall scales	
OHT measuring scales	
Dynamic Geometry software (e.g. *Cabri, Geometer's Sketchpad*)	Reasoning
Interlocking cubes	Building shapes, exploring volume and surface area, enlargements
Small mirrors	Symmetry
Balance scales, weights and modelling clay	
Various jugs of different capacities	
Clocks and timetables	
Platonic solids pack	Recognising 3D shapes
A variety of very large 2D shapes (at least 30 cm high)	Hide and reveal activity, where part of the shape is hidden and gradually revealed as children try to identify the shape

Data handling and probability

Equipment	Some possible uses
Dice, coins	Probability
Probability pots (based on DIME probability kits)	Probability
Spreadsheet/Database	Data handling

Other

Equipment	Some possible uses
Mini-whiteboards, pens and wipes	Rapid assessment of pupils' understanding Calculations, diagrams
Posters	In each of the topic areas, to support discussion
Games	Counting, recognising numbers on dice, probability, developing strategies, shape recognition, use of co-ordinate grids (e.g. Battleships) Calculations (e.g. 24 game)

Dotty activities

Resources – 3 × 3; 4 × 4; 5 × 5 squared dotty paper; full-page squared dotty paper, isometric dotty paper

1) Equivalent perimeters

Objectives: Recognise perpendicular and parallel lines. Identify right angles. Find perimeters of shapes. Apply understanding of perimeter to reason about shapes.

Activity

What shapes can you draw on 4 × 4 dotty paper, using only perpendicular lines? Find the perimeters of your shapes.

Key questions

How many of them have a perimeter of 12 cm?
Why do the cross and the square (3 cm × 3 cm) have the same perimeter?
Which type of shape has a different perimeter?
Which shape has the largest perimeter?
What are the angles inside the shapes?

2) Square areas

Objectives: Find areas of squares, by counting, and by geometric reasoning.

Activity

Using 5 × 5 dotty paper, how many different squares can you draw?
(There are eight: four aligned vertically, four 'skewed'. Note that many children would wish to call the skewed squares, diamonds. But they are still squares.)

Key questions

What are the areas of these squares?
What are the lengths of the sides of your squares?
Tabulate your results, showing side length and area.
The numbers 1, 4, 9, 16 are known as square numbers. Why? Why not the others?
Why can't you make an area of three squares on this paper?

3) Shapes on dotty paper

Objectives: Make shapes with increasing accuracy; find reflective symmetry in regular polygons; classify quadrilaterals.

Activity

On 4×4 dotty paper, can you draw all these?

a) Five different sized squares?

b) A rhombus (not a square)?

c) Nine different parallelograms?

d) How many different rectangles?

e) How many different kites?

f) How many different trapezia?

g) As many different isosceles triangles as you can

Key questions

Can you show the lines of symmetry on these shapes?

Can you find the areas of each of these?

What makes a rhombus different from a parallelogram or from a square?

How many of these shapes could be drawn on 3×3 dotty paper?

3 × 3 dotty paper

4 × 4 dotty paper

5 × 5 dotty paper

Sources list

Supplier	Contact	Resources
ATM 7 Shaftesbury Street Derby DE23 8YB	Phone 01332 346599 Fax 01332 204357 Email admin@atm.org.uk Website www.atm.org.uk	Points of departure Exploring Middles Tiles and tiling MAT tiles Algebra and number Jigsaws, Puzzles, Developing Number software Active Geometry software Linking Cubes Proof Maths activities for Special children Posters
BEAM BEAM Education Maze Workshops 72a Southgate Road London N1 3JT	Order 020 7684 3330 General 020 7684 3323 Fax 020 7684 3334 email info@beam.co.uk website www.beam.co.uk	Credit cards Place value money cards Customised dice Probability pots, dice, counters and beans OHP materials Number line paper
Chartwell-Yorke Ltd 114 High Street Belmont Village Bolton, Lancashire BL7 8AL	Tel: 01204 811001 Fax: 01204 811008 Email info@chartwellyorke.com Web www.chartwellyorke.com	Maths software and associated books – e.g. Cabri
Education Initiatives Geoff Faux Cardew Farm Dalston Carlisle CA5 7JQ	Tel: 01228 710661 Fax: 01228 711090	Multiplication charts, 100 squares Place value charts
Invicta Plastics Ltd Harborough Road Oadby Leicester LE2 4LB	Tel: 0116 272 0555 Fax: 0116 272 8393	Geostrips – shape construction equipment
Learning Development Aids (LDA) Duke Street, Wisbech Cambridgeshire PE13 2AE	Tel: 01945 463 441	Mathsteps assessment and teaching programme
Learning Resources 5 Merchants Close Oldmedow Road King's Lynn, Norfolk PE30 4JX	Tel: 01553 762276 Fax: 01553 769943 Email: euroinfo@learning-resources.co.uk Website: www.learning resources.com	

Supplier	Contact	Resources
The Mathematical Association 259 London Road Leicester LE2 3BE	Tel: 0116 221 0013 Fax: 0116 244 8508 Website: www.m-a.org.uk	Books of ideas for teachers
Median Publications The Dryll, Llanarmon DC Wrexham CB, LL20 7LF	Tel: 01691 600643	MEDIAN algebra Handling data Number packs
Polydron International Ltd Kemble, Cirencester Gloucestershire GL7 6BA	Tel: 01285 770055 Email: HeadOffice@Poldron.com Website: www.polydron.com	Shape construction equipment
Shell Centre Shell Centre, School of Education, University of Nottingham, Jubilee Campus, Nottingham NG8 1BB, UK	Tel: 0115 951 4410 Fax: 0115 951 4413 Email: Information@MathShell. com Website: www.mathshell.com	Language of functions and graphs Patterns with problems and numbers Numeracy through problem-solving Research
SMILE Distribution and Publications c/o York Distribution Services 64 Hallfield Road Layerthorpe York YO31 7ZQ	Tel: 0190 443 1218 Fax: 0190 443 0868 Email: info@smilemathematics. co.uk Website: www.smilemathematics. co.uk	Publications
SMILE Software Isaac Newton Centre 108a Lancaster Road London W11 1QS	Tel: 020 7598 4841 Fax: 020 7598 4838 Email: info@smilemathematics. co.uk Website: www.smilemathematics. co.uk	Software
SummuS UK Ltd 21–23 Clifton Road Rugby Warwickshire CV21 3PY	Tel: 01788 551441 Fax: 01788 551270 Email: summusuk@aol.com	24-game
Tarquin Publications Stradbroke, Diss Norfolk IP21 5JP	Tel: 01379 384218 Fax: 01379 384289	DIME Probability Algebra through Geometry Posters, books Maths equipment
TTS Nunn Brook Road Huthwaite Nottinghamshire NG17 2HV	Tel: 01623 447888 Website: www.tts-group.co.uk	OHT acetates

A writing frame for a data handling task

My hypothesis is _____

(Your hypothesis could begin with the words 'I believe that . . .' or 'My opinion is that . . .')

Planning and data collection

To find out if my hypothesis is correct, I am going to collect some data. The data I intend to collect is _____

_____

_____

This is how I am going to collect my data: _____

_____

_____

Presentation

To record my results, I am going to use _____

_____

To present my results, I am going to use _____

_____

because _____

_____

_____

Calculations

I will need to make the following calculations: _____

_____

_____

Conclusion

My hypothesis was true/false/not proven, because _____

_____

_____

Evaluation

What further data should I collect? _____

_____

_____

What other calculations could I make? _____

_____

Were my presentations the most effective I could have chosen?

_____

What others could I have used? _____

Interpreting graphs and charts in lesson starters

What is wrong?

Year	%
1999	0.1
2000	0.2
2001	0.25
2002	0.32
2003	0.38

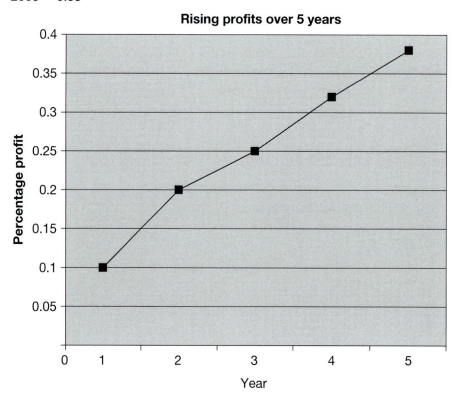

What is wrong?

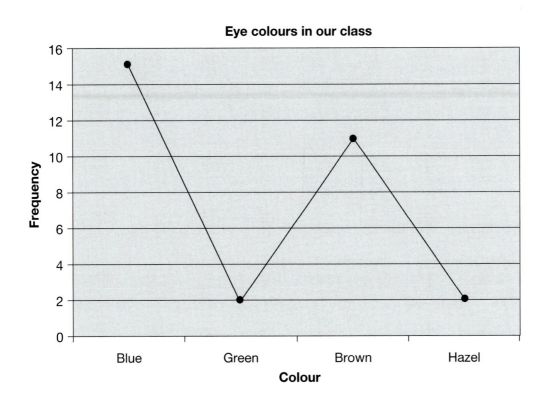

Questions in mathematics, using Bloom's taxonomy (1956)

Focus	Possible questions
Knowledge	What is the special name of this quadrilateral? What is the product of 8×6?
Comprehension	Explain how we calculate . . . Describe the shape in this picture.
Application	What shape of graph do you expect? Can you predict . . .
Analysis	Should the lines on this graph reach the axes? Can you break this problem down into smaller steps? What does this data tell us?
Synthesis	Can you find a rule for this generalisation? Can you predict the next number in the sequence? Can you predict the 10th number? What if we didn't have brackets in this calculation?
Evaluation	Which calculation method is better in this case? Is this data valid? Did you choose to collect the right data? What errors are there in this diagram/chart/graph?

Linking equations

Using the spider diagram to find links between equations

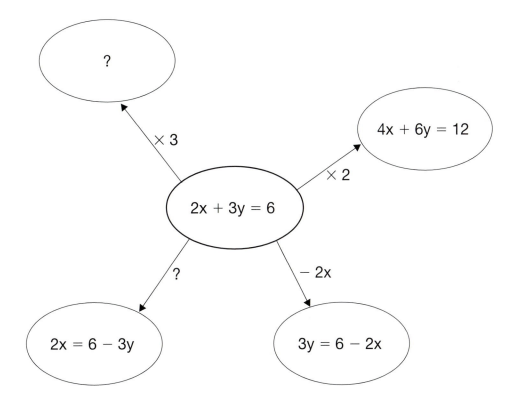

Children could be invited to fill in the blanks – whether inside the ellipses or to find the links.

The idea could be extended so that only the outside ellipses contain information, and the pupils have to deduce the centre of the spider.

A writing frame for problem-solving

Understanding and representing the problem – recognising problem types and organising relevant information	I have to find out . . . The information I can use is . . .
Selecting or planning the solution – breaking the problem into steps and reviewing alternative strategies	The other information I have to find is . . . I will use . . . Any other calculations I need to make would be . . . I will present my results, using . . .
Executing the plan – carrying out routines, such as calculations	I found out that . . .
Evaluating results – reviewing and making sense of answers	I can check my answer by . . .

Translating Key Concepts for children who experience difficulties with mathematics, into objectives illustrated by the National Framework documents (Primary and Key Stage 3)

Key Concept	Translated into National Curriculum levels and teaching objectives	Possible progression	Related Key Stage 3 Objectives
Number, including cardinality and ordinality	P8: Begin to recognise numerals from 1 to 9 and relate them to sets of objects. P8: Begin to use ordinal numbers (first, second or third) when describing position of objects, people or events.	Level 1: Say and use the number names in order in familiar contexts.	
Counting, including one-to-one correspondence	P6: Understand one-to-one correspondence in a range of contexts. P8: Begin to count up to ten objects. Level $\frac{1}{2}$: Count reliably at least 20 objects.	Level 2: Count, read, write and order whole numbers to at least 100; know what each digit represents (including 0 as a place holder).	

Key Concept	Translated into National Curriculum levels and teaching objectives	Possible progression	Related Key Stage 3 Objectives
Operation of combining and partitioning	Level 2: Use mental strategies to solve simple problems using counting, addition, subtraction, doubling and halving, explaining methods and reasoning orally. Level 2: Use knowledge that addition can be done in any order to do mental calculations more efficiently.	Level 3: Use known number facts and place value to add or subtract mentally, including any pair of two-digit whole numbers. Level 4: Mental calculation strategies: partition.	Y7: Consolidate and extend mental methods of calculation to include decimals, fractions and percentages, accompanied where appropriate by suitable jottings; solve simple word problems mentally.
Comparing two numbers/quantities	P7: Use familiar words to compare size and quantity. P8: Compare directly two lengths or heights, where the difference is marked and can indicate 'the long one' or 'the tall one'. Level 1: Use language such as 'more' or 'less', 'greater' or 'smaller', 'heavier' or 'lighter', to compare two numbers or quantities. Level 1: Compare two lengths, masses or capacities by direct comparison.	Level 3: Estimate, measure and compare lengths, masses and capacities, using standard units; suggest suitable units and equipment for such measurements. Level 3: Read, write and order whole numbers to at least 1000; know what each digit represents. Level 4: Order a given set of positive and negative integers.	Y7: Compare and order decimals in different contexts; know that when comparing measurements they must be in the same units.

Key Concept	Translated into National Curriculum levels and teaching objectives	Possible progression	Related Key Stage 3 Objectives
Concepts of length, mass, capacity, time and money	P8: Show awareness of time through some familiarity with names of the days of the week and significant times of the day. Level 2: Suggest suitable standard or uniform non-standard units and measuring equipment to estimate, then measure, a length, mass or capacity.	Level 3: Use units of time and know the relationships between them (second, minute, hour, day, week, month, year). Level 4: Know and use the relationships between familiar units of length, mass and capacity.	Y8: Use units of measurement to estimate, calculate and solve problems in everyday contexts.
Shape: Classification of 2D and 3D shapes Classification by criteria Concept of having properties or attributes	Level 1: Use everyday language to describe features of familiar 3D and 2-D shapes. Level 2: Use the mathematical names for common 2D and 3D shapes; sort shapes and describe some of their features.	Level 3: Classify polygons, using criteria such as number of right angles, whether or not they are regular, symmetry properties.	Y7: Begin to identify and use angle, side and symmetry properties of triangles and quadrilaterals; solve geometric problems involving these properties, using step-by-step deduction and explaining reasoning with diagrams and text.
Mathematical pattern (shape, number, handling data)	P8: Recognise, describe and recreate simple repeating patterns and sequences. P8: Describe shapes in simple models, pictures and patterns. Level 1: Talk about, recognise and recreate simple patterns.	Level 2: Describe and extend simple number sequences (including odd/even numbers, counting on or back in ones or tens from any two-digit number, and so on).	Y7: Generate sequences from practical contexts and describe the general term in simple cases. Y8/9 Interpret tables, graphs and diagrams for both discrete and continuous data, and draw inferences that relate to the problem being explored. Have a basic understanding of correlation.

Key Concept	Translated into National Curriculum levels and teaching objectives	Possible progression	Related Key Stage 3 Objectives
Handling data: Concept of having properties or attributes Classification by criteria	P7: Identify when an object is different and does not belong to a given familiar category.	Level 3: Solve a given problem by organising and interpreting numerical data in simple lists, tables and graphs.	Y7: Plan how to collect and organise small sets of data; construct frequency tables for discrete data, grouped where appropriate in equal class intervals.
Position, direction and movement	Level 1: Use everyday words to describe position. Level 2: Use mathematical vocabulary to describe position, direction and movement.	Level 4: Recognise where a shape will be after reflection or translation. Level 4: Read and plot co-ordinates in the first quadrant.	Y7: Recognise and visualise the transformation and symmetry of a 2D shape. Y7: Find co-ordinates of points determined by geometric information (all four quadrants). Y8: Solve problems involving angles and bearings.
Complements to 'useful' numbers, e.g. 10, 100, 1000 and multiples of these; also to 0.1 and 1 when calculating with decimals	Level 2: Know by heart all pairs of numbers with a total of 10. Level 2: Use knowledge that addition can be done in any order to do mental calculations more efficiently.	Level 3: Find any pairs of numbers with a total of 100. Level 4: Extend to pairs of numbers with a total of 1. Level 3: Use known number facts and place value to add or subtract mentally, including any pair of two-digit whole numbers.	Y7: Consolidate and extend mental methods of calculation.

Key Concept	Translated into National Curriculum levels and teaching objectives	Possible progression	Related Key Stage 3 Objectives
Place value, linked with the effect of multiplying by 10, 100, 1000 and decimal fractions	Level 2: Within the range 0 to 30, say the number that is 1 or 10 more or less than any given number. Level 3: Count on or back in tens or hundreds from any two- or three-digit number. Level 3: Add and subtract mentally a near multiple of 10 to or from a two-digit number.	Level 3: Round any positive integer less than 1000 to the nearest 10 or 100. Level 4: Multiply and divide any positive integer up to 10 000 by 10 or 100 and understand the effect. Level 5: Multiply and divide decimals mentally by 10 or 100, and integers by 1000, and explain the effect.	Y7: Understand and use decimal notation and place value; multiply and divide integers and decimals by 10, 100, 1000 and explain the effect.
Multiples – the times tables	Level 2: Know by heart facts for the 2, 5 and 10 multiplication tables.	Level 3: Know by heart facts for the 2, 3, 4, 5 and 10 multiplication tables.	Y7: Multiply and divide three-digit by two-digit whole numbers; extend to multiplying and dividing decimals with one or two places by single-digit whole numbers.

Key Concept	Translated into National Curriculum levels and teaching objectives	Possible progression	Related Key Stage 3 Objectives
The relationships between the four arithmetic operations, and the links to algebra	Level 2: Understand the operation of addition, and of subtraction (as take away or difference), and use the related vocabulary. Level 2: Understand that subtraction is the inverse of addition; state the subtraction corresponding to a given addition and vice versa. Level 3: Understand the operation of multiplication as repeated addition or as describing an array. Level 3: Know and use halving as the inverse of doubling.	Level 3: Understand division and recognise that division is the inverse of multiplication. Level 3: Derive quickly division facts corresponding to the 2, 3, 4, 5 and 10 multiplication tables.	Y7: Know and use the order of operations. Y7: Understand that algebraic operations follow the same conventions and order as arithmetic operations.
Using appropriate vocabulary to describe mathematical situations	P7: Respond appropriately to key vocabulary and questions.	Level 3: Explain methods and reasoning, orally and in writing.	Y7: Present and interpret solutions in the context of the original problem, explain and justify methods and conclusions.

Key Concept	Translated into National Curriculum levels and teaching objectives	Possible progression	Related Key Stage 3 Objectives
Problem-solving: **Understand the problem** • Extract information • Represent the problem mathematically (e.g. translate the problem into diagrams) **Plan the solution** • Identify the necessary information to solve the problem • Break the problem down into simpler steps, work systematically • Choose and use appropriate operations and methods **Technical fluency** • Carry out the calculations **Checking, evaluating** • Check and evaluate solutions • Explain results and conclusions	Level 2: Choose and use appropriate operations and efficient calculation strategies to solve problems, explaining how the problem was solved. Level 3: Solve a given problem by organising and interpreting numerical data in simple lists, tables and graphs.	Level 4: Use all four operations to solve simple word problems involving numbers and quantities, including time, explaining methods and reasoning. Level 5: Solve a problem by extracting and interpreting information presented in tables, graphs and charts.	Y7: Solve word problems and investigate in a range of contexts; compare and evaluate solutions. Y7/8: Identify the necessary information to solve a problem; represent problems mathematically. Y7: Break a complex calculation into simpler steps. Y7: Choose and use appropriate and efficient operations and methods.

An example of an individual pupil assessment sheet, based on some Key Concepts and Objectives

Key Concept	Translated into National Curriculum levels and teaching objectives	Possible progression	Related Key Stage 3 Objectives	Assessment and comments
Number, including cardinality and ordinality	P8: Begin to recognise numerals from 1 to 9 and relate them to sets of objects. P8: Begin to use ordinal numbers (first, second or third) when describing position of objects, people or events.	Level 1: Say and use the number names in order in familiar contexts.		
Counting, including one-to-one correspondence	P6: Understand one-to-one correspondence in a range of contexts. P8: Begin to count up to ten objects. Level 2: Count reliably at least 20 objects.	Level 2: Count, read, write and order whole numbers to at least 100; know what each digit represents (including 0 as a place holder).		

Key Concept	Translated into National Curriculum levels and teaching objectives	Possible progression	Related Key Stage 3 Objectives	Assessment and comments
Operation of combining and partitioning	Level 2: Use mental strategies to solve simple problems using counting, addition, subtraction, doubling and halving, explaining methods and reasoning orally. Level 2: Use knowledge that addition can be done in any order to do mental calculations more efficiently.	Level 3: Use known number facts and place value to add or subtract mentally, including any pair of two-digit whole numbers. Level 4: Mental calculation strategies: partition.	Y7: Consolidate and extend mental methods of calculation to include decimals, fractions and percentages, accompanied where appropriate by suitable jottings; solve simple word problems mentally.	
Comparing two numbers/ quantities	P7: Use familiar words to compare size and quantity. P8: Compare directly two lengths or heights, where the difference is marked and can indicate 'the long one' or 'the tall one'. Level 1: Use language, e.g. 'more'/'less', 'greater'/ 'smaller', 'heavier'/'lighter', to compare two numbers or quantities. Level 1: Compare two lengths, masses or capacities by direct comparison.	Level 3: Estimate, measure and compare lengths, masses and capacities, using standard units; suggest suitable units and equipment for such measurements. Level 3: Read, write and order whole numbers to at least 1000; know what each digit represents. Level 4: Order a given set of positive and negative integers.	Y7: Compare and order decimals in different contexts; know that when comparing measurements they must be in the same units.	

Key Concept	Translated into National Curriculum levels and teaching objectives	Possible progression	Related Key Stage 3 Objectives	Assessment and comments
Concepts of length, mass, capacity, time and money	P8: Show awareness of time through some familiarity with names of the days of the week and significant times of the day. Level 2: Suggest suitable standard or uniform non-standard units and measuring equipment to estimate, then measure, a length, mass or capacity.	Level 3: Use units of time and know the relationships between them (second, minute, hour, day, week, month, year). Level 4: Know and use the relationships between familiar units of length, mass and capacity.	Y8: Use units of measurement to estimate, calculate and solve problems in everyday contexts.	
Shape: Classification of 2D and 3D shapes Classification by criteria Concept of having properties or attributes	Level 1: Use everyday language to describe features of familiar 3D and 2D shapes. Level 2: Use the mathematical names for common 2D and 3D shapes; sort shapes and describe some of their features.	Level 3: Classify polygons, using criteria such as number of right angles, whether or not they are regular, symmetry properties.	Y7: Begin to identify and use angle, side and symmetry properties of triangles and quadrilaterals; solve geometric problems involving these properties, using step-by-step deduction and explaining reasoning with diagrams and text.	

Key Concept	Translated into National Curriculum levels and teaching objectives	Possible progression	Related Key Stage 3 Objectives	Assessment and comments
Mathematical pattern (shape, number, handling data)	P8: Recognise, describe and recreate simple repeating patterns and sequences. P8: Describe shapes in simple models, pictures and patterns. Level 1: Talk about, recognise and recreate simple patterns.	Level 2: Describe and extend simple number sequences (including odd/even numbers, counting on or back in ones or tens from any two-digit number, and so on).	Y7: Generate sequences from practical contexts and describe the general term in simple cases. Y8/9: Interpret tables, graphs and diagrams for both discrete and continuous data, and draw inferences that relate to the problem being explored. Have a basic understanding of correlation.	
Handling data: Concept of having properties or attributes Classification by criteria	P7: Identify when an object is different and does not belong to a given familiar category.	Level 3: Solve a given problem by organising and interpreting numerical data in simple lists, tables and graphs.	Y7: Plan how to collect and organise small sets of data; construct frequency tables for discrete data, grouped where appropriate in equal class intervals.	

Key Concept	Translated into National Curriculum levels and teaching objectives	Possible progression	Related Key Stage 3 Objectives	Assessment and comments
Position, direction and movement	Level 1: Use everyday words to describe position. Level 2: Use mathematical vocabulary to describe position, direction and movement.	Level 4: Recognise where a shape will be after reflection or translation. Level 4: Read and plot co-ordinates in the first quadrant.	Y7: Recognise and visualise the transformation and symmetry of a 2D shape. Y7: Find co-ordinates of points determined by geometric information (all four quadrants). Y8: Solve problems involving angles and bearings.	
Complements to 'useful' numbers, e.g. 10, 100, 1000 and multiples of these; also to 0.1 and 1 when calculating with decimals	Level 2: Know by heart all pairs of numbers with a total of 10. Level 2: Use knowledge that addition can be done in any order to do mental calculations more efficiently.	Level 3: Find any pairs of numbers with a total of 100. Level 4: Extend to pairs of numbers with a total of 1. Level 3: Use known number facts and place value to add or subtract mentally, including any pair of two-digit whole numbers.	Y7: Consolidate and extend mental methods of calculation.	

Key Concept	Translated into National Curriculum levels and teaching objectives	Possible progression	Related Key Stage 3 Objectives	Assessment and comments
Place value, linked with the effect of multiplying by 10, 100, 1000 and decimal fractions	Level 2: Within the range 0 to 30, say the number that is 1 or 10 more or less than any given number. Level 3: Count on or back in tens or hundreds from any two- or three-digit number. Level 3: Add and subtract mentally a 'near multiple of 10' to or from a two-digit number.	Level 3: Round any positive integer less than 1000 to the nearest 10 or 100. Level 4: Multiply and divide any positive integer up to 10 000 by 10 or 100 and understand the effect. Level 5: Multiply and divide decimals mentally by 10 or 100, and integers by 1,000, and explain the effect.	Y7: Understand and use decimal notation and place value; multiply and divide integers and decimals by 10, 100, 1000 and explain the effect.	
Multiples – the times tables	Level 2: Know by heart facts for the 2, 5 and 10 multiplication tables.	Level 3: Know by heart facts for the 2, 3, 4, 5 and 10 multiplication tables.	Y7: Multiply and divide three-digit by two-digit whole numbers; extend to multiplying and dividing decimals with one or two places by single-digit whole numbers.	

Key Concept	Translated into National Curriculum levels and teaching objectives	Possible progression	Related Key Stage 3 Objectives	Assessment and comments
The relationships between the four arithmetic operations, and the links to algebra	Level 2: Understand the operation of addition, and of subtraction (as take away or difference), and use the related vocabulary. Level 2: Understand that subtraction is the inverse of addition; state the subtraction corresponding to a given addition and vice versa. Level 3: Understand the operation of multiplication as repeated addition or as describing an array. Level 3: Know and use halving as the inverse of doubling.	Level 3: Understand division and recognise that division is the inverse of multiplication. Level 3: Derive quickly division facts corresponding to the 2, 3, 4, 5 and 10 multiplication tables.	Y7: Know and use the order of operations. Y7: Understand that algebraic operations follow the same conventions and order as arithmetic operations.	

A partially completed pupil record sheet

Achievements could be indicated in a number of ways – by highlighting achieved objectives, or by indicating partial achievement through different colours (red, amber, green) or numbers (1 – not achieved, 2 – partial achievement, 3 – achieved)

Pupil name: A. N. Other   **Year: 7**

Key Concept	Translated into objectives	Possible progression	Related Key Stage 3 Objectives	Assessment and comments
Complements to useful numbers – 10, 100, 1000 and their multiples; also to 1 when calculating with decimals	Level 2: Know by heart all pairs of numbers with a total of 10. Level 2: Use knowledge that addition can be done in any order to do mental calculations more efficiently.	Level 3: Find any pairs of numbers with a total of zx100 Level 4: Extend to pairs of numbers with a total of 1. Level 3: Use known number facts and place value to add or subtract mentally, including any pair of two-digit whole numbers.	Y7: Consolidate and extend mental methods of calculation.	Adding and subtracting mentally, but only with 2D and 1D numbers, rather than 2 2D numbers.
Place value, linked with the effect of multiplying by 10, 100, 1000 and decimal fractions	Level 2: Within the range 0 to 30, say the number that is 1 or 10 more or less than any given number. Level 3: Count on or back in tens or hundreds from any two- or three-digit number. Level 3: Add and subtract mentally a 'near multiple of 10' to or from a two-digit number.	Level 3: Round any positive integer less than 1000 to the nearest 10 or 100. Level 4: Multiply and divide any positive integer up to 10 000 by 10 or 100 and understand the effect. Level 5: Multiply and divide decimals mentally by 10 or 100, and integers by 1000, and explain the effect.	Y7: Understand and use decimal notation and place value, multiply and divide integers and decimals by 10, 100, 1000 and explain the effect.	Can add or subtract mentally when the number is near 10, e.g. 8, 9, 11 or 12. Will try adding 21, 31, 41, etc. next.

Key Concept	Translated into objectives	Possible progression	Related Key Stage 3 Objectives	Assessment and comments
Multiples – the times tables	Level 2: Know by heart facts for the 2, 5 and 10 multiplication tables.	Level 3: Know by heart facts for the 2, 3, 4, 5 and 10 multiplication tables.	Y7: Multiply and divide three-digit by two-digit whole numbers; extend to multiplying and dividing decimals with one or two places by single-digit whole numbers.	*Still working on the 3x table. Can attempt grid method of multiplying 2D x 2D numbers, simple digits.*
The relationships between the four arithmetic operations, and the links to algebra	Level 2: Understand the operation of addition, and of subtraction (as 'take away' or 'difference'), and use the related vocabulary. Level 2: Understand that subtraction is the inverse of addition; state the subtraction corresponding to a given addition and vice versa. Level 3: Understand the operation of multiplication as repeated addition or as describing an array. Level 3: Know and use halving as the inverse of doubling.	Level 3: Understand division and recognise that division is the inverse of multiplication. Level 3: Derive quickly division facts corresponding to the 2, 3, 4, 5 and 10 multiplication tables.	Y7: Know and use the order of operations. Y7: Understand that algebraic operations follow the same conventions and order as arithmetic operations.	*Doubling is fine, but finds difficulty with halving, even with small numbers. Maybe work using cubes in two rows, showing how 2 x 5 = 10, so that $\frac{1}{2}$ of 10 = 5. Try with a range of numbers.*

An example of a self-assessment sheet for pupils

Key objectives and traffic lights – a self-assessment sheet for pupils to keep and refer to regularly

Key Concept	Objective	Self-assessment Red = I really don't understand this Amber = not sure Green = confident		
		Red	Amber	Green
Number, including cardinality and ordinality	Say and use the number names in order in familiar contexts.			
Counting, including one-to-one correspondence	Count, read, write and order whole numbers to at least 100; know what each digit represents (including 0 as a place holder).			
Operation of combining and partitioning	Use known number facts and place value to add or subtract mentally, including any pair of two-digit whole numbers. Mental calculation strategies: partition.			
Comparing two numbers/ quantities	Estimate, measure and compare lengths, masses and capacities, using standard units; suggest suitable units and equipment for such measurements. Read, write and order whole numbers to at least 1000; know what each digit represents.			

Key Concept	Objective	Self-assessment Red = I really don't understand this Amber = not sure Green = confident		
		Red	Amber	Green
Concepts of length, mass, capacity, time and money	Use units of time and know the relationships between them (second, minute, hour, day, week, month, year). Know and use the relationships between familiar units of length, mass and capacity.			
Shape: Classification of 2D and 3D shapes Classification by criteria Concept of having properties or attributes	Classify polygons, using criteria such as number of right angles, whether or not they are regular, symmetry properties.			
Mathematical pattern (shape, number, handling data)	Describe and extend simple number sequences (including odd/even numbers, counting on or back in ones or tens from any two-digit number, and so on).			
Handling data: Concept of having properties or attributes Classification by criteria	Solve a given problem by organising and interpreting numerical data in simple lists, tables and graphs.			
Position, direction and movement	Recognise where a shape will be after reflection or translation. Read and plot co-ordinates in the first quadrant.			
Complements to 'useful' numbers, e.g. 10, 100, 1000 and multiples of these; also to 0.1 and 1 when calculating with decimals	Find any pairs of numbers with a total of 100. Use known number facts and place value to add or subtract mentally, including any pair of two-digit whole numbers.			

Key Concept	Objective	Self-assessment Red = I really don't understand this Amber = not sure Green = confident		
		Red	Amber	Green
Place value, linked with the effect of multiplying by 10, 100, 1000 and decimal fractions	Round any positive integer less than 1000 to the nearest 10 or 100. Multiply and divide any positive integer up to 10000 by 10 or 100 and understand the effect.			
Multiples – the times tables	Know by heart facts for the 2, 5 and 10 multiplication tables.			
The relationships between the four arithmetic operations, and the links to algebra	Understand that subtraction is the inverse of addition; state the subtraction corresponding to a given addition and vice versa. Know and use halving as the inverse of doubling.			
Using appropriate vocabulary to describe mathematical situations	Explain methods and reasoning, orally and in writing.			
Problem-solving: **Understand the problem** • Extract information • Represent the problem mathematically (e.g. translate the problem into diagrams) **Plan the solution** • Identify the necessary information to solve the problem • Break the problem down into simpler steps, work systematically • Choose and use appropriate operations and methods **Technical fluency** • Carry out the calculations **Checking, evaluating** • Check and evaluate solutions Explain results and conclusions	Choose and use appropriate operations and efficient calculation strategies to solve problems, explaining how the problem was solved. Solve a given problem by organising and interpreting numerical data in simple lists, tables and graphs.			

Examples of IEP targets, strategies and achievement criteria

Key Concept Areas of difficulty	Objectives/targets	Strategies including resources, staff, time	Achievement criteria	Assessment
Shape: Classification of 2D and 3D shapes Classification by criteria Concept of having properties or attributes	Classify polygons, using criteria such as number of right angles, whether or not they are regular, symmetry properties.	Lessons to include: building/ drawing shapes from given criteria (using interlocking strips, dotty paper). Tessellating shapes (ATM mats, drawings) – which shapes tessellate and why? Guessing shapes games, e.g. children sit back to back and describe shapes for others to draw.	Can explain the difference between two quadrilaterals given in diagrams, using appropriate vocabulary. Can draw or make triangles or quadrilaterals from given criteria.	
Mathematical pattern (shape, number, handling data)	Describe and extend simple number sequences (including odd/even numbers, counting on or back in ones or tens from any two-digit number, and so on).	Main activities in lessons: Create number sequences from physical patterns, e.g. using interlocking cubes, counting the numbers of cubes used in each shape in a sequence. Change the resources, e.g. sticks for creating patterns in shapes.	Uses patterns in numbers to predict later numbers in sequence – Odd numbers Even numbers Counting in tens from any number, e.g. 12, 22, 32, etc. Counting in fives from any number, e.g. 1, 6, 11, etc.	

Key Concept Areas of difficulty	Objectives/Targets	Strategies including resources, staff, time	Achievement criteria	Assessment
Complements to 'useful' numbers, e.g. 10, 100, 1000 and multiples of these; also to 0.1 and 1 when calculating with decimals	Find any pairs of numbers with a total of 100.	Use computer software package – registration times, TA supporting. Lesson starters: Counting stick activities 100 square Number lines	Can discuss methods for solving any calculation to find two numbers which sum to 100.	
Handling data: Concept of having properties or attributes Classification by criteria	Solve a given problem by organising and interpreting numerical data in simple lists, tables and graphs.	Starters to include discussion of examples of incorrectly drawn charts. Main activities for lessons develop number sequences, organise the numbers into tables. Use Mathematics Challenge (DfES 0200/2003) – section 7 on reading charts. TA to spend Monday registration times using this resource – three sessions initially.	Can organise information from number sequence activities into a table, can find a pattern in the number sequences, can predict later outcomes.	

Generic GCSE criteria, written for pupils

Marks 1 to 8 relate to the range of GCSE grades G–A*, but the relationship is not exact. One mark in each strand (therefore a total of 3 marks) would not be sufficient to attain a G Grade. A candidate attaining grade G would be expected to have a total of 5 marks across the three strands.

Mark	Strand 1 Making and monitoring decisions	Strand 2 Communicating mathematically	Strand 3 Developing skills of mathematical reasoning
1	I try different ways of solving the problem. I organise my work and check results.	I begin to explain my thinking, and discuss my work. I use and interpret maths symbols and diagrams.	I show an understanding of a general statement.
2	I use mathematical methods for solving problems, e.g. use a tally chart or a graph.	I present information and results in an organised way (e.g. a table) and explain the reasons for my presentation.	I search for a pattern by trying ideas of my own.
3	I can choose the information I need to solve the problem. I check to see that my results are sensible.	I describe situations mathematically, perhaps by using words, symbols and diagrams.	I make up my own general statements – rules – based on evidence of my own work.
4	I solve complex problems by breaking them down into smaller, simpler tasks.	I can use and explain a range of tables, charts, diagrams, words and symbols when presenting my findings.	I can show that the rules I have found work by testing some examples.
3	I can choose the information I need to solve the problem. I check to see that my results are sensible.	I describe situations mathematically, perhaps by using words, symbols and diagrams.	I make up my own general statements – rules – based on evidence of my own work.

Mark	Strand 1 Making and monitoring decisions	Strand 2 Communicating mathematically	Strand 3 Developing skills of mathematical reasoning
4	I solve complex problems by breaking them down into smaller, simpler tasks.	I can use and explain a range of tables, charts, diagrams, words and symbols when presenting my findings.	I can show that the rules I have found work by testing some examples.
5	I can extend the original problem by introducing new lines of enquiry.	I can give reasons why I have chosen a particular way to present my results.	I can explain the rules I have found by looking at the mathematical structure of the situation. I show I understand the difference between experimental evidence in a few cases and a full explanation.
6	I develop and follow my own approaches to the problem. These are fully explored and checked.	I use symbols consistently to explain my mathematical ideas.	I can explain how I obtained my rules, and how they helped me to progress with the problem.
7	I can examine new methods introduced with my work, and give detailed reasons why I am using them.	I can use symbols and mathematical language accurately.	My report includes mathematical justifications explaining my solutions to problems involving a number of features or variables.
8	I have considered and evaluated a number of approaches to a task, and explored a new maths area.	I have used symbols, mathematical language and graphical information in an efficient and effective way.	I can provide a proof of my solution to a complex problem, considering the conditions under which it remains valid.

Commentary for using the compass roses (Appendix 8.2)

Bearings

Each rose may be used as OHTs or drawn on the board. If the arrowed line is indicated with a 0°, then the class can be asked the values at each of the arms.

Patterns can be explored, e.g. 90°, 180°, 270°, 360°; or in the second diagram, 60°, 120°, 180°, etc.

Relationships can also be explored, e.g. if the angle shown at the end of one arm is 45°, what angle is at the other end of the line? (225°). We can make explicit that the difference between these angles is always 180°.

The OHTs can be placed at different orientations (so that north does not always have to face up to the top of the page), to develop children's capacity to identify bearings, and their understanding that the bearing is related to north (0°).

Differences between the angles may also be explored, e.g. what is the difference between 135° and 225°?

Each of these activities develops children's visual imagery – the answer to the last problem is 90°, but is readily confirmed when children 'see' the solution.

Compass roses

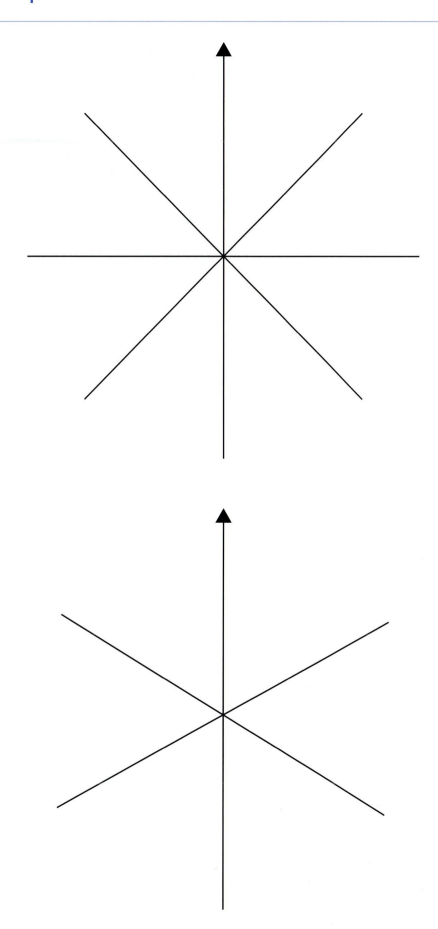

References

Berger, A., Morris, D. and Portman, J. (2000) *Implementing the National Numeracy Strategy for Pupils with Learning Difficulties.* London: David Fulton.

Black, P. (1999) 'Assessment, Learning Theories and Testing Systems' in Murphy, P. (ed.) *Learners, learning and assessment.* London: The Open University (Paul Chapman Publishing).

Black, P. and Wiliam, D. (1998) *Inside the Black Box.* London: King's College.

Bloom, B. S. and Krathwohl, D. (1956) *Taxonomy of educational objectives: the classification of educational goals.* Handbook 1: *Cognitive domain.* Addison Wesley.

Bruner, J. (1996) *The Culture of Education.* Cambridge, MA/London: Harvard University Press.

Buckley, S. and Bird, G. (1993) 'Teaching children with down's syndrome to read', *Down's Syndrome: Research & Practice* **2**(2): 47–50.

Corbett, J. and Slee, R. (2000) 'An international conversation on inclusive education' in Armstrong, F., Armstrong, D. and Barton, L. (eds) *Inclusive Education: Policy, Contexts and Comparative Perspectives.* London: David Fulton.

DfES (1999) *Framework for teaching mathematics – Reception to Year 6.* London: DfES Publications.

DfES (2001) *Framework for teaching mathematics – Years 7, 8 and 9.* London: DfES Publications.

DfES (0292/2002) *Accessing the National Curriculum for Mathematics – Examples of what pupils with special educational needs should be able to do at each P Level.* London: DfES Publications.

Fox, G. and Halliwell, M. (2000) *Supporting Literacy and Numeracy – A guide for Teaching Assistants.* London: David Fulton.

Gardner, H. and Boix-Mansilla, V. (1994) 'Teaching for understanding in the disciplines and beyond,' *Teachers College Record,* **96**(2): 198–208, 216–17.

Greeno, J. G., Pearson, P. D. and Schonenfield, A. H. (1997) 'Achievement and theories of knowing and learning' in McCormick, R. and Paechter, C. (eds) *'Learning and Knowledge'.* London: The Open University (Paul Chapman Publishing).

Hart, S. (2000) *Thinking Through Teaching.* London: David Fulton.

Kay, J. and Yeo, D. (2003) *Dyslexia and Maths.* London: David Fulton.

Lave, J. and Wenger, E. (1991) *Situated Learning: Legitimate Peripheral Participation.* Cambridge: Cambridge University Press.

Lever, M. (2003) *Activities for children with mathematical learning difficulties – Number, Shape and Space, Measures and Handling Data.* London: David Fulton.

Lorenz, S. (1998) *Children with Down's Syndrome.* London: David Fulton.

McDermott, R. P. (1993) 'The acquisition of a child by a learning disability' in Chalikin, S. and Lave, J. (eds) *Understanding Practice: Perspectives on Activity and Context*: 269–95. New York: Cambridge University Press.

MacGrath, M. (1998) *The Art of Teaching Peacefully.* London: David Fulton.

McNamara, S. and Moreton, G. (1997) *Understanding Differentiation – A Teacher's Guide.* London: David Fulton.

Mason, J.H. (1988) *Learning and Doing Mathematics.* Basingstoke/London: MacMillan.

Murphy, P. (1998) 'Supporting Collaborative Learning: a gender dimension' in Murphy, P. (ed.) *Learners, learning and assessment.* London: The Open University (Paul Chapman Publishing).

Ollerton, M. (2003) *Everyone is Special.* Derby: Association of Teachers of Mathematics.

Prestage, S. and Perks, P. (2001) *Adapting and Extending Secondary Mathematics Activities – New Tasks for Old.* London: David Fulton.

Rogoff, B. (1998) 'Cognitive Development Through Social Interaction: Vygotsky and Piaget' in Murphy, P. (ed.) *Learners, learning and assessment.* London: The Open University (Paul Chapman Publishing).

Stakes, R. and Hornby, G. (2000) *Meeting Special Needs in Mainstream Schools* (2nd edn). London: David Fulton.

Vygotsky, L. S. (1962) *Thought and Language.* Cambridge, MA: MIT Press.

Wiske, M. S. (1998) 'What is Teaching for Understanding?' in M. S. Wiske (ed.) *Teaching for Understanding. Guide: Linking Research with Practice.* San Francisco: Jossey-Bass.